UNIVERSITY SUCCESS FORMULA

Your Step-by-Step Guide to Excelling in University and Life

Dr. Jasmine Filion

Published by Jasmine Filion Education, Calgary, Alberta

Cover and Interior Design: Jasmine Filion Education

Editor: Rhonda Fleming

Publication Assistance and Digital Printing in Canada.

ISBN 978-0-9940207-0-3

For more information, visit www.UniversitySuccessFormula.com

EARLY PRAISE FOR UNIVERSITY SUCCESS FORMULA

"This book is a real gold mine for any freshman college student. It should even be read at the end of high school and then reread throughout their studies."

– Yolande Blanchette

"Through her book, Jasmine shares with students all the tools they will need to succeed."

– Alain Caron

"If I had only known and applied a tenth of the information contained in this book, I could have saved myself half of my study time!"

– Dr. Edith Boulanger

"What a joy to have a book that allows our children to become successful students and, later on, accomplished young professionals."

– Michel Filion

"If you read only one book on how to succeed in your studies, this is the one!"

– Jean Normandeau

"This is probably the best book available on college success."

– Marie-Chantal Couillard

"This is an excellent book, full of practical applications that every college student needs!"

– Rhonda Fleming

"This will undoubtedly be the favorite reference book of any university student who reads it."

– Alexandre Lemay

"What a chance to learn from the wisdom of a successful graduate student!"

– Hilda Flores Picazo

"The strategies in this book are practical, easy to apply and really paid off!"

– Joël Filion

"This is the book that you must have if you are going to college."

– Sophie Martin

"The advice in this book will help the average student become one of the best students."

– Dr. Shaelyn Pham

“So many students are confused and not well-prepared for college. Reading this book will get them started on the right foot from day one!”

– Anne-Marie Samson

“If I had read this book before starting my studies, I would have been able to immediately implement strategies to help me perform my best.”

– Jean Filion

“It’s a shame I didn’t benefit from this book when I was in college!”

– Dr. Marie-Joëlle Bronsard

ACKNOWLEDGEMENTS

I want to thank my lovely husband Simon-Pierre Caron for his endless patience and wonderful encouragement while I wrote this book.

I also want to thank my close friends and family for sharing with me their wisdom and some of their college experiences: Jean Filion, Joel Filion, Cynthia Labrecque, Marie-Joëlle Bronsard, Edith Boulanger and Alexandre Lemay.

I also want to thank my inspiring friend, Dr. Hélène Michaud, for her perseverance, her positive outlook, her authenticity, her joy and her strong belief in this project. She continues to motivate and inspire me every day.

Finally, I want to thank my wonderful editor, Rhonda Fleming, who did an amazing job making sure every single word in this book is relevant and meaningful.

CONTENTS

WHY I HAD TO WRITE THIS BOOK

Hello! My name is Jasmine Filion and I'm the author of this book.

I live in Calgary in the province of Alberta in western Canada.

I got my college degree in natural sciences at 18 years of age at Merici College in Quebec. And I got my university degree in dental medicine when I was 22 years old at Laval University in Quebec City.

Here in Quebec, students can go to "college" at the approximate age of 16. These are typically technical, applied arts or applied sciences schools where students study for two years. Then they can go to university to get a more specialized degree.

The dental medicine program is one of the most difficult and intense courses of study at our university in Quebec. I remember attending 14 classes a week during the winter session in my third year. It was a crazy schedule!

During my years of postsecondary education, I worked hard, but I also made a lot of mistakes. Fortunately, I learned from most of them. With persistence, I managed to graduate first in my college at Merici and at the top of my class in dental medicine at Laval.

I also tutored other students and led study groups while completing my education. I noticed that the successful students possessed different habits and attitudes than those who were struggling. I also noticed particular characteristics in the students who later succeeded in their careers as opposed to those who didn't do as well.

After graduation, I realized that I had learned how to study successfully and that I also knew what to focus on while studying so I could later enjoy a great career. Actually, my mentees–the students I have tutored–helped me realize this. They're the ones who told me I had to share my strategies with the world!

Not only do my mentees tell me that they wish they had known these tips before starting college, but I wish I had known them, too! The reality is that no student knows how to succeed in college and university. That is a subject that is not usually taught. Some students are lucky enough to discover it through hard work and mistakes. But others discover it too late or never.

In my case, I learned many secrets about how to succeed through a lot of trial and error, and in the end, I did very well. Now I am enjoying a very nice career where I continue to discover more of those success secrets every single day.

And you know what? You can, too!

And I want you to! That is why I wrote this book.

Read it. Put the principles into practice. And you, too, can have a happy, balanced, and successful student life and a great career!

HOW TO USE THIS BOOK

This is not a book you will read through one time, learn everything you need to know, put it back on the shelf and forget about it.

This is a book you will refer to numerous times during your studies.

The methods described in this book are simple, proven, and feasible for any college student to execute. They are easy to understand and ready for you to apply. They're described in order and offer you a real step-by-step recipe you can follow for success.

Obviously this book is for future college students as well as current students, but it is especially for those individuals who want to be successful in their studies, earn a degree, and have a fabulous career one day.

I also suggest that parents read this book if you have a child going off to college. It will help you understand the vast differences between high school and college and the stress that can accompany those differences. It will also help you encourage your children to apply these principles so they can be successful students.

<u>How to use the principles presented here:</u>

I encourage you to read and adopt the principles in this book for a variety of reasons. The main reason is to learn how to be successful at college. You learned a lot of things during your primary and secondary education, but you probably didn't learn how to learn, and I believe that is one big reason why so many students drop out of college.

Another reason is that, if you need a college degree, your time in college is a crucial factor in the success of your career. And you typically won't get a second chance if you make irreparable mistakes during your studies. Use the principles in this book to avoid costly mistakes and learn how to be an exceptional student and go on to have the career you're dreaming of.

If you succeeded brilliantly in high school and think you'll just breeze through college, you're in for a surprise. College is much more difficult than high school. You'll soon discover that some of your old habits, like only studying the night before an exam, won't work. By reading this book, you'll be able to learn the best success tips to apply in college.

If you're already in college and running out of time to do what you have to do, this book can save you a lot of time, much more than you can even imagine. Use these principles to make changes now, before it's too late.

How to read this book:

To get started, I suggest you read this book from beginning to end. That will give you an overview of what it covers and a better understanding of the content.

Then, when you need specific information on a topic, go to the table of contents, find the principle you're looking for, and go directly to that subject.

I also suggest you read the table of contents regularly during each semester to remind you of the main principles you need to adopt.

How to use the Reminders list:

I have also added a list of Reminders in the back of the book. These are the 17 most important principles in this book. These particular principles are marked with this symbol * in the Table of Contents at the beginning of the book, in the Contents list at the beginning of each Part, as well as when each principle is presented in detail. I suggest reading through the Reminders list on a weekly basis and reading the description of each of those principles a few times during each semester.

<u>How to apply principles to different types of students:</u>

The principles needed to be a successful student are available to everyone. But all students don't have the same learning style and each student is following a unique path. So, although the principles in this book are logical, all of them may not apply to everyone. Each student must apply the principles that correspond to her maturity and her personality.

For instance, perhaps you're a very creative student who daydreams in class, but produces tons of ideas for solving problems. One of the principles in this book encourages students to develop their creativity. Obviously, because you're already very creative, you don't necessarily need to develop any more creativity. Instead, you may need to develop other aspects that will help you be more successful.

Or perhaps you're a shy student, who mainly works alone, spending most of your time separated from the group. One of the principles of this book suggests developing your leadership skills and taking responsibility within a group. It will probably be more difficult for you to take responsibility within a group compared to another student who is a natural leader. However, it would be good for you to get involved in your community and spend some time out of your comfort zone.

So don't worry if you have difficulty applying certain principles. Remember, every student is different and will have different principles that they excel in and others that are more difficult to master. Ultimately, these principles are there to help you balance your strengths and improve your weaknesses. The more you master the principles in this book, the more successful you will be.

Also, some students will read certain principles and think they're "obvious" truths everyone should already know. Other students will not think those particular principles are so "obvious" but will have a different set that they think everyone should have already adopted. And most adults will think that the majority of the principles I've shared in this book should be "obvious" to practically everyone.

The truth is, everyone's life experience is different, and that means the lessons each one has learned are different from everyone else's. So just because some of the principles are already a natural part of your study habits, there are a lot of other principles in this book that you probably need to learn.

And parents, remember that you've lived through a lot more life experiences than your children have. So don't assume they already know and understand and are putting into practice the majority of these principles. That's why they need to read this book and start adopting these success secrets now.

INTRODUCTION

"An encyclopedic knowledge and a prodigious memory are not guarantees of success in life. What matters is the understanding a few key ideas and their implementation."

Bob Proctor

Congratulations! If you're spending your valuable time reading this book, I assume you are in college or are planning to go to college and possibly even further in your education. And more exciting than that is the fact that you want to make your time in college as successful as possible.

Your success during your post-secondary education is dependent on three variables: your habits, your skills and your attitude. The *University Success Formula* that I've developed and that I'll share with you in this book looks like this:

UNIVERSITY SUCCESS = HABITS + SKILLS + ATTITUDE

Your **habits** are the actions that you do regularly to move closer to your goals. It may be starting early to study for an exam and getting up at the same time every day. Your **skills** are the abilities you possess that make your actions effective and efficient. For example, being organized and communicating properly. Your **attitude** is your way of being and thinking. This is, among other things, your confidence and positive outlook.

You must have all three ingredients in order to have the winning recipe for University Success.

You may well have the attitude and the habits, but if you don't have the right skills, you won't succeed. Even if you really want to become an engineer and are very creative, your chances of success will be very slim if you haven't learned to think logically.

Or if you have incredible skills and an exemplary attitude but don't have good habits, you won't be successful. A student who wants to become a true athlete must not only be naturally good in sports and show great determination, but he must also practice his sport regularly. Without excellent habits, he won't be a great athlete.

And you can have great skills and good habits, but if you don't have the right attitude, you still won't be successful. A very bright student who is a hard worker usually won't do well in her interview for the job of her dreams if she lacks self-confidence.

So to succeed, it takes good habits, good skills and the right attitude. But that's not all. These three elements must be applied in all three areas that characterize college life:

- Academic environment
- Extracurricular activities
- Workplace

Those three different areas were also highlighted by Patrick S. O'Brien, in his book *"Making College Count: A Real World Look at How to Succeed In and After College."*

As you'll learn in this book, your post-secondary education is not confined to academics or activities in the classroom. It also includes the extracurricular activities outside of class in which a student can–and should–be involved. This could be participating on a sports team or serving on a committee or in an organization or club.

Your education also includes your work experience. Some students work during the school year and/or during the summer. It could be a paid or unpaid internship or a paid summer job. It can also be participating in volunteer work. Or you could be a student who decides to start his own business.

Why do you need to be involved in all three areas? So you can develop not only theoretical knowledge but also practical knowledge. And even more importantly, so you can develop all the necessary skills for a successful career. Academics will help to develop certain recognized skills, but your extracurricular activities and your experience in the workplace will develop others that are just as necessary.

Together, your experience in those three different areas will allow you to develop yourself on all levels in college. They will help you become accomplished and balanced, develop a winning attitude, possess the best skills and practice excellent habits.

This book presents my *University Success Formula:* these three variables (habits, skills, attitude) applied in the three educational arenas (academics, extracurricular, work). Each variable is broken down into simple principles, in order, and ready to be applied.

My formula for university success is presented in a step-by-step, easy-to-use format. As you read, if you notice that some ideas are repeated, pay close attention to them. They are extremely important.

Remember, the most important principles in this book are marked with this symbol * in the Table of Contents of the book, in the Contents list at the beginning of each Part, and when these principles are discussed in detail. I have also included a list of these particular principles in the back of the book. It's titled Reminders.

It's time to get started! Turn the page and start your journey down the road to success!

PART ONE: SET YOUR GOALS

"Goals are dreams with a deadline."

Napoleon Hill

In order for the university success formula to work for you, you need to determine what your goals are for your college experience. Part One will help you discover exactly which goals you want to reach.

Your goals will represent your personal definition of a successful college experience. It could include objectives like:

- Getting and maintaining a scholarship every year.
- Graduating in the top 5% of your class.
- Receiving two honorary awards at graduation for your community involvement.
- Having a job offer from one of your top three employment choices before you graduate.
- All of the above.

You have to know what your objectives are in order to know whether or not you're on the road to success. And you need to determine which goals you want to meet so you can determine what actions you need to take in order to achieve them.

The process of determining goals for your college experience is your responsibility. And in order to help you fulfill that responsibility, you need to know–or take steps to find out–who you are, who you want to be, and what profession will be the most fulfilling to you.

And that's what Part One will help you discover.

Part One Contents

1. Be Responsible*

Responsibility is the power to make decisions for yourself and accepting the consequences of those decisions, whether they are positive or negative.

Why is being responsible the first thing on our list?

- Because going to college generally marks the transition from adolescence into adulthood.
- Because no one can study for you, no one can decide your career for you, and no one can live your life for you.

How can you be responsible?

First, make decisions for your own life. Others can give you advice about the different paths you may choose to take, but the final decision is all yours. Blindly accepting what your parents or friends think is best for your life is delegating your responsibility to someone else. But even that is a choice you make, and you are the one who will be living with the consequences.

Second, accept the consequences of your decisions and your actions. Let's say you made a commitment to complete your part of your team's project work by November 17. But you procrastinated until the last minute because you were too busy having fun and enjoying your new freedom. Now the deadline is here and your part of the work isn't complete. You will have to accept the consequence of having some very upset teammates who probably won't choose you for their team again. And you'll probably get a lower grade on the project than you were anticipating.

Another way to accept the consequences of your decisions is to recognize when you have made a mistake. For example, you may realize that you made the wrong decision when choosing your major or your career path. That is what Edith, one of my friends, did. Here's what she told me:

> *Since I was a little girl, I have loved dentistry. But when it came time to choose a profession I would be involved in for the rest of my life, I just wasn't sure which one to choose. When I started college, I was interested in everything! But I knew I wanted to be active and do something more than sit on my butt in front of a computer all day.*
>
> *So I decided to go into physiotherapy. That would keep me active during the day. I really liked sports, so I thought I would love it. But after my second year I started doubting my decision. And after my third year I realized I couldn't see myself doing that all my life. I realized that what I really wanted to do was to be a dentist.*
>
> *Since I was so close, I went ahead and finished my degree in physical therapy. Then I went into dentistry.*
>
> *I've always taken the responsibility for that mistake. I made a poor career choice by not going directly into dentistry.*

Another way to be responsible is to stop blaming other people or events for what happens to you. You are responsible for your failures as well as your successes. If you partied the night before a final exam and failed the exam, you are responsible and you are the only one to blame. But if you studied for your test, went to bed early and aced the exam, you are the one responsible and you should congratulate yourself!

2. Discover Who You Are

Self-discovery is learning what your values, your strengths, your passions, and your weaknesses are. Don't worry if you can't immediately list all of these traits. This discovery process is often the work of a lifetime. Through a variety of life experiences, you will get to know yourself better and better. But, for now, just focus on what you already know.

Why do you need to discover who you are?

- Because you have to determine who you are today before you can decide who you want to become in the future.
- To make sure you stay true to, and be honest with, yourself.
- To decide what work you need to do to become the person you want to be.
- To determine the factors influencing your productivity and how to use them to your advantage.
- To know what your main types of intelligence are and how to make the most of them.

How do you find out who you are?

Determine your values, strengths, weaknesses and passions.

A first step toward self-discovery would be to determine your values, your strengths, your weaknesses and your passions. In my case, my values include respect, kindness and authenticity. My strengths are my great manual dexterity, an artistic eye and a scientific mind. My weaknesses are my English (but I'm working on it!) and my shyness. My passions are science, art and working with my hands. How about you? What are your values, strengths, weaknesses and passions?

Determine the factors that affect your productivity.

A second step would be to determine what the circumstances are that maximize and minimize your productivity. If you want to study effectively, you should know the time of day and the type of place where you are the most productive. You should also know the amount of sleep that you need to perform at your maximum, as well as the kind of food that allows you to be at your peak performance. You should also know what things hurt your efficiency.

Knowing which factors influence your productivity allows you to use them to your advantage by optimizing the favorable factors and minimizing the unfavorable ones. If you are more productive in the morning after seven hours of sleep and more productive studying on campus rather than in your dorm or apartment, then it is in your best interest to plan to sleep about seven hours each night, get up early and go study on campus before your classes begin.

This is a concept that Marie, another friend of mine, understood:

> *I'm really a morning person, so I study during the morning hours. For example, this weekend I went to the library on Saturday morning at 8 and I didn't leave there until noon. During the week, I usually arrive on campus very early, studying about an hour in the morning before my classes begin. It's rare that I do any studying at night because I'm tired and not able to concentrate. If I do any coursework at night, it might be to do some assigned readings or review my notes while watching TV.*

Determine your intelligence types.

A third thing that will help you discover who you are is to determine what kind of intelligence you have. As mentioned by Professor Michael Geison in *"How to Become A SuperStar Student,"* Howard Gardner explained seven types of intelligence: visual, kinesthetic, musical, social, reflective, logical and linguistic.[1]

Do you like to see things in order to understand them better? Do you have a vivid imagination? Do you like to write and draw pictures? Then you probably have a visual intelligence.

Do you like to move a lot and participate in sports? Do you like to build things and use your hands and your body? You probably have a kinesthetic intelligence.

Or perhaps you love to sing, write songs, create melodies and listen to music? Then you may have a musical intelligence.

Do you like interacting with people, supporting and helping others? Are you often the tutor or leader in a group? Do you prefer to study with friends? You could have a social intelligence.

Conversely, do you prefer to study alone and do your own assignments in a quiet place? If so, the reflective intelligence seems to characterize you.

But that's not all! Do you like to analyze and work with numbers? Do you like to create links and associations between several things? You probably have a logical intelligence.

Finally, perhaps you have a linguistic intelligence. This is the case if you like reading, writing, speaking and working with words. This is also the case if you like to communicate the information and transmit it to others.

By knowing your main types of intelligence (yes, most people have a combination of these seven types), you can use them to your advantage to learn more effectively. For example, if you have a linguistic intelligence, sharing with others what you learn could really benefit you. So getting involved in study groups may be a good idea for you. Or, for example, if you have a logical intelligence, creating links between different topics you're studying and organizing your ideas could really help you study effectively.

Similarly, if you have a reflective intelligence, you would probably learn better alone. But if you're social, you would learn best by interacting with others, in a study group, for example. If you have musical intelligence you might learn better listening to music. And if you're a visual person, seeing, writing and drawing what you learn could really benefit you.

And if you are kinesthetic, you'd better move while you are studying. This may be gesturing, mimicking or doing something like bouncing a ball off the wall to occupy your hands.

You get the idea. And don't forget: the majority of you have more than one type of intelligence. So you are smart!

3. Find Out Who You Want to Be and Choose a Profession

Discovering who you want to become in life may be a continually active process, just like discovering who you are. You may already have an idea of what you would like to become, but that could change in a few years or even after a specific event. This is normal, so don't be surprised if your self-discoveries evolve over time.

While it is perfectly normal not to know today exactly who you want to become, it is not recommended that you wait for a great idea or inspiration to hit you, or for a life-changing event to happen, before you make a career choice. If necessary, find someone, such as an academic advisor, to help guide you.

It is important to make a decision, take action and keep going, even if you're not exactly sure where you want to end up. If you determine at some point in the future (say, next week or next year) that you've taken the wrong path, then you've discovered one thing you don't want to be involved in for the rest of your life, and you can definitely eliminate that choice. Of course, it would be great to choose the right path on the first try, but if that doesn't happen, don't keep going down the wrong path. Immediately choose another path and continue moving forward.

Why do you need to discover who you want to be and choose a profession?

- To determine your goals which will give meaning to your life.
- To define success for yourself.
- To decide if you really need to go to college.
- To determine how to reach your goals.

How do you discover who you want to become and choose a profession?

<u>Be honest.</u>

First, be honest with yourself. You need to become the person you want to become, not the person your family or friends want you to become. Your parents definitely want you to be happy. But be careful not to live their dream or practice the profession they wish they had chosen for themselves.

<u>Determine your life's SMART goals.</u>

Next, determine your life's goals. Ask yourself who you want to become and what you want to accomplish in your life. I recommend you set goals in all areas of your life: education, work, family, hobbies, finance, health, and spirituality. This diversified approach will help you develop fully and have a balanced life.

Also, to help you identify your goals, I suggest you follow the SMART principle. This principle states that a good goal is Specific (it must be exact), Measurable (you must be able to calculate your progress), Ambitious (it must be a challenge), Realistic (it must be possible) and Time-based (it must have a deadline). For example, a SMART goal for you may be: "I am going for a walk outside at least 25 minutes a day."

<u>Select a profession.</u>

After you've set goals in all areas of your life, then ask yourself, "What professions will allow me to achieve my goals? What are the professions that will allow me to use my strengths, work on my passions, be happy, continue to grow as a person, and live a fulfilling life?" To help you decide, consider spending a day with a professional working in a field that interests you. This will give you a better idea of what his work life is really like and it may help you be able to confirm or eliminate a career choice.

Decide on your field of study.

Next, determine if you need to go to college to achieve your goals. If not, don't! Instead start achieving your goals now. If you do need to go, consider the majors that are related to the various professions that interest you and investigate the different colleges that offer those majors. If you don't know what you're interested in, don't hesitate to ask for help from someone, for example, an academic advisor.

If you still don't know which major to commit to, you may want to choose a less specialized program or take courses in a variety of programs. Or consider taking some classes in the program that interests you the most. By the end of your first semester or your first year, you may know which programs interest you more. The important thing is to make a decision for now and try something, even if it means changing programs later on. The experience you gain will always be beneficial and the knowledge you gain will never be wasted.

It is a fact that a lot of students change their majors. Cynthia is a friend of mine who changed programs. Here is her experience:

> *I always wanted to be an elementary school teacher. So I chose that as my major when I started college. At the end of my first year, I did an internship for one week in an elementary school and it was a nightmare! During that week I decided that teaching elementary school was NOT what I wanted to do!*
>
> *So I changed majors and took the courses required to be a nursing assistant for elderly people. I want to help people and this age group appealed to me more. I have*

learned that taking care of elderly people, making them laugh, getting them to smile at me, receiving a thank you from them or just having the personal satisfaction of helping them is very rewarding to me. This profession is where I belong.

Discover your school.

When you have decided what you want to major in, look for schools that offer your major course of study. Some programs have a limited number of spaces and can require interviews or additional exams. You'll need to pay close attention to all deadlines and prerequisites during your application process.

Once you've been accepted to your chosen college and your major course of study, start learning more about your college environment. Check out the extracurricular activities that are available. What student organizations are you interested in? What are the internship opportunities in your major that you can apply for? What work opportunities of interest are available on and off campus?

Set your college SMART goals.

Then, spend some time determining the goals that you are going to pursue and would like to reach by graduation. I suggest using the SMART method again. Decide who you want to be by the time you graduate. What skills do you want to develop by then? What attitudes and habits do you want to have adopted?

Also, determine what accomplishments you want to achieve during your college days. And this isn't just about academics. It's also involvement in extracurricular activities as well as experience in the workplace. In fact, in order to have a balanced life, I strongly suggest you develop yourself in all three areas: academics, extracurricular activities, and work experience. For example, one of your goals may be: "At my graduation ceremony, I want to get at least two awards for my community involvement."

Achieve success.

Finally, after you've determined your goals for your time as a student, realize that these represent your personal definition of your college success. I encourage you to write them down, display them in your room, and visualize yourself having achieved them every day. The more you visualize them, the stronger they become in your mind and the closer you get to their achievement. And as I mentioned earlier, remember that your interests and passions may change over time, so review your goals after each semester and adjust them as needed.

PART TWO: DISCOVER THE WORLD OF COLLEGE

"I have never let my schooling interfere with my education."

Mark Twain

Welcome to the wonderful world of college!

And congratulations, too, because I assume you have probably been accepted - or soon will be - into your chosen program. Admission is one step closer to graduation!

In Part Two, you will discover the differences between college and high school, as well as the main problems you may encounter in college. You will also discover the importance of taking control of your education and how you can adapt to major changes.

Part Two Contents

4. Differentiate Between College and High School

This section is to help you realize and understand the differences between college and high school.

Why do you need to understand the differences?

- Because students have not been adequately informed about the differences between college and high school and have not been trained to deal with them.
- Because these differences can be the source of shock, confusion, stress, anxiety, depression or exhaustion for some students.
- To understand the challenges you will face as a college student and to be prepared to deal with them.
- To understand the necessity for you to adapt to college.

How is college different than high school?

<u>More Freedom</u>

First, I'm sure you're looking forward to the fact that college life includes greater freedom and less supervision. That's because you're now considered a responsible adult. This freedom means that you have the power to do what you want with your time and with your actions. I'm sure you're thinking–how exciting!! But it's a danger, too. You're free to spend your time working hard and taking the steps necessary to prepare you to have an extraordinary career. But that means you're also free to do the opposite.

Some habits, such as irresponsible drinking, drug consumption, and irresponsible sex, can harm you and others and can endanger your career. You can decide to have a good time partying on weekends and neglecting to adequately study for your exams. But when you see your transcripts and realize you didn't pass all your courses and won't graduate, you'll probably realize that the good time you had in the short-term wasn't worth the price you'll be paying in the long run. Looking back you'll realize that graduating in your field of study with good grades and a good reputation would have been worth missing a few parties.

More Work

Second, college classes involve a greater workload: more notes, more readings, more study material, more work. Plus the courses and exams are longer and more complex. And while your workload increases, your other obligations are not reduced and your available time is not increased. It's no surprise that college students often feel overwhelmed by their workload.

More Stress

Third, college involves more stress. The workload can cause anxiety. The presence of a larger number of students per class and the presence of a greater need to perform and distinguish yourself from the rest of the class also contributes to anxiety. In some cases, stress is good. But more often than not, it has a negative effect and reduces your efficiency. Later in this book I will discuss some excellent ways to reduce your stress before and after exams. These techniques can be used at other times as well.

More Difficulties

Finally, understand that most of the difficulties college students face are related to the management of their time and priorities, management of their workload, and management of their stress. A difficult financial situation may also present a significant challenge. The principles outlined in this book will help you manage your time, your workload, your stress and much more.

Here's what Alex, a mechanical engineering student, shares about the differences between high school and college:

> *What I've realized is that in high school I didn't have as much work to do during the semester. And most of my grade was earned from my mid-term and final exams. And because the amount of work wasn't great, I was able to do very well just by studying a little for exams, often at the last minute. That was easy to do in high school.*
>
> *But if I want to perform well in college, I can't wait until the last minute, because I have a lot of work to do throughout the semester. In fact, I have long reports due about every 2-3 weeks. So I have to make a sustained effort and really plan my schedule in advance in order to get all my work accomplished.*
>
> *I have also realized that in college I'm the one with my foot on the gas pedal. If I want to take more courses per semester, I can. I have more latitude, a greater freedom to load up my semester schedule as much as I am able to take.*
>
> *So the biggest difference is in time management. In high school, there was a pace imposed on me and I was able to study at the end of the semester and still get good grades. But in college, a large portion of my grade is based on assignments I have to turn in throughout the semester.*
>
> *So I have to manage my schedule in order to get everything done on time. And if I want to have a bigger workload, I can. I am considered an adult. There is no one holding my hand. That's the big difference.*

5. Control Your Education*

Education is learning that occurs throughout life. It includes all the knowledge, skills and life experiences that you learn over time.

Why do you need to control your education?

- To make sure you have a diversified and balanced education.
- To decide what you really want to learn.
- To see learning as a pleasure, not a chore.
- To reduce your stress.

How do you control your education?

<u>Get a Diversified Education</u>

First, acknowledge the importance of having a diversified and balanced education. College focuses mainly on academics. And that's totally normal. But college is just one part of your education. In the classroom you learn to memorize and understand theory. Academics will help you develop certain skills: hard work, logic, organization and critical thinking. Those skills will allow you to succeed in your individual work and get good grades. Then those grades will help you get a job interview.

The other part of your education–which is a major part of your life–is obtained outside the classroom. It is done in extracurricular activities and working environments. There you learn to really communicate, to work in a team environment, to be creative and, most importantly, to be practical. Extracurricular activities and working environments promote and allow you to develop a number of other skills, such as leadership, teamwork and communication.

Those skills allow you to excel when working on a team and to develop the necessary skills to help you get the job you want.

Alex, the student in mechanical engineering, has been involved in the SAE (Society of Automatic Engineer) and the aerospace group in his school. He found that extracurricular activities bring him a practical approach:

> *These activities help me learn a very necessary aspect of life–the aspect of teamwork. Getting experience in teamwork while in college is very helpful because teamwork is always harder than we think. Just learning to work as part of a team, as well as managing a team, gives you good practical skills that you will use on your job.*

While academics is important, it's only one part of your education. Giving it 100% of your time and energy doesn't allow you to be practical or to develop all the skills you will need to be successful in your career. So be sure you also invest some of your time and energy in extracurricular activities and working environments. This will also help you be happier and have a more balanced life.

Focus on Essential Information

You also need to realize that you can't learn everything. Knowledge is infinite. When starting college, some students fall into the trap of trying to learn all their course material in detail. Even if that was possible in high school, it's impossible in college. Admitting that you can't learn everything allows you to reduce your stress and save some energy.

So be discerning. Make a decision about what you really want to learn. Since you can't learn all the material taught at college, you should choose what you'll learn. In fact, you should learn what you really want to learn, what will be the most helpful for your career, what will help you on your exams, and what will make you happy. Focus on the information that you determine to be essential. In Part Three, you will discover how to determine which study material is essential.

6. Be Ready to Adapt to Changes

The entry into the college world is a significant life change. To survive and to blossom with this major change, you must adapt.

Why do you need to adapt to college life?

- To survive to it, to blossom through it and to excel in it.

How do you adapt to college life?

1. Recognize that entering college is an important change. Remember some of the differences we talked about between college and high school? More freedom, less supervision, greater workload, more stress, more internship and work opportunities, larger campus, larger selection of courses, larger classes, more choices of extracurricular activities, etc.

2. Recognize that to survive and thrive following a major change, you must adapt. And to adapt means to improve or change some of your ways of doing things or of thinking. For example, in high school you were probably used to being criticized by your teachers if you didn't turn in your work on time. But in college, no one will criticize you if your work is not turned in on time. This is why you need to learn to discipline yourself.

Another example could be your study habits. If in high school you used to start studying for your exams the day before and did pretty well, your study habits will need to change in college. You will have a lot of lecture notes and readings to deal with in order to be prepared for an exam, so you won't be able to succeed by only studying the night before the exam. You will need to start studying much earlier than you're used to.

3. I encourage you to start adapting to college now - even if you're not there yet. Based on what you now know about college, ask yourself what habits you already know that need improving, what skills you could develop more and what part of your attitude you could change. For example, it could be you need to be more self-disciplined or more organized. And don't worry if you don't know yet all the aspects you may need to improve or change. Simply start thinking about it. You'll discover the best habits, skills and attitudes to develop further on in this book.

Obviously, the adaptation required is different for every single person. Here is an example from Alex, the mechanical engineering student:

> *In college, nobody forces you to go to class. If I didn't want to go to class, I didn't go. But in order to learn what I needed to know and to do my best work, I needed to show up for class.*
>
> *But I wasn't going to all my classes because I lived too far away from campus. And since I wasn't going to class, I was missing the explanations the professor was giving in class to explain the difficult parts of the study material.*
>
> *Over time, I realized that it's much easier when the teacher explains the study material in class rather than to try and learn it by myself from the textbook. I also realized that I wasn't saving myself time by not going to class and later spending a lot of time trying to understand the material by myself.*
>
> *So I moved close enough to the campus that I could walk to class.*
>
> *It's one of the things I had to adapt to in order to increase my attendance in class and learn what I needed to learn.*

7. Avoid Believing These Myths

Like anything else, there are some myths about college. And I recommend that you don't fall into the trap of believing them.

Why do you need to avoid believing these myths?

- To ensure that you know the truth about college life.
- To understand what will really contribute to your success.

What are these myths?

- *"A college degree guarantees you a job after graduation."*

A college degree can increase your chances of finding a job, but it doesn't necessarily ensure that you'll get a job. Employers today are looking for more than prospects with a college degree. They are looking for individuals with the skills and attitude that will contribute to the success of their businesses.

- *"A college degree guarantees you a better job."*

A degree can help you find a better job, but it doesn't guarantee that you'll get the best one. Competition is very high in the workplace. Employers almost always prefer employees who possess the skills and attitude that will help their businesses succeed. They also prefer those who have the right contacts and references from people they trust.

- *"Having a high GPA guarantees you a better job."*

This is wrong for the same reasons. In addition to grades, employers want employees with multiple skills and a winning attitude. And those who have some connections with their prospective employers have an advantage over those who don't.

- *"Only the super smart kids go to college."*

Today anyone can take college courses. College offers a wide choice of majors and courses of study that cover the interests and strengths of everyone. And remember, everyone is intelligent. We just don't all share the same kind of intelligence.

- *"You have to be a 'party animal' or you won't make any friends."*

This is obviously not true. There are a lot of ways to make friends at college without having to participate in all of the 'welcome' parties, club initiations and other activities for freshman students.

A lot of incoming students believe they have to participate in all of those activities or parties in order to make friends at college. But you don't. Your decision to attend those events is your choice. There are a lot of freshman students who don't go. So if you don't go, you won't be the only one. Plus, there are a lot other ways to make friends, like getting involved with a student committee or joining a club.

But if you do choose to attend any of those events, be careful. Some of them present opportunities that can escalate very quickly to irresponsible behavior. In these cases, it may be better to avoid those particular events totally. Use your best judgment.

PART THREE: PRACTICE THE BEST HABITS

"We are what we repeatedly do. Excellence, then, is not an act, but a habit."

Aristotle

The first variable to achieving success in college is your habits. Habits are essential. They give you the concrete actions you need to perform regularly so you can succeed.

These habits are presented in the following areas in which they apply:

- Every day
- Before-during-after classes
- Before-during-after exams
- In extracurricular activities
- In the workplace

Are you ready? Let's go. This is the longest part of the book, but the easiest to read. And if you are a "practical" student, you will find this part particularly interesting.

Part Three Contents

28. Set Deadlines for Your Tasks
29. Start Assignments Immediately
30. Read Each Day's Class Notes that Night*
31. Determine What the Essential Study Material Is
32. Select Key Material for the Rereading of Your Notes*
33. Select Key Material for the Rereading of Your Assigned Readings
34. Decide If Your Reading Assignments are Worth Your Time*
35. Do Your Readings in a Way that Serves Your Purpose
36. Understand the General Content of Your Classes*
37. Escape to a Secret Location Every Week*
38. Study in Blocks of 50 Minutes
39. Plan Each Week's Schedule on Sunday Night

Before Exams

40. Anticipate What Will Be on Your Exam*
41. Study in the Way that Works Best for You
42. Memorize Early, Regularly and Effectively
43. Consider Using a Study Group
44. Review Your Key Material the Day Before and the Morning of the Exam
45. Reduce Your Stress Before Your Exam

During Exams

46. Skim Through Your Exam
47. Use Good Test-Taking Strategies*
48. Guide Your Team to Complete All Teamwork
49. Finish Your Written Work a Few Days in Advance
50. Practice Your Oral Presentation
51. Prepare for Your Practical Exam

After Exams

Every Day

The habits that are listed here should be done every day to really maximize your productivity, your health and your life balance during your time in college.

8. Visualize Your Goals*

In one of the previous principles, I invited you to identify, write down and visualize your goals regularly. This is very effective–especially the visualization part. In fact, the more you visualize your goals, the more your subconscious mind works for you to help make them happen. In addition, your conscious mind will help you remember to stay focused on your goals. Visualization is a well-known method for achieving goals.

Why do you need to visualize your goals?

- Because the more you visualize them, the closer you get to achieving your goals.

How do you visualize your goals?

Take a few minutes each day to remind yourself of your goals. Then imagine that you have accomplished your goals. What do you see? What do you hear? How do you feel? Use all of your senses to imagine what your life is like when you have accomplished your goals.

9. Eat Well

Eating well means eating mainly nutritious foods, in reasonable quantities, at reasonable times and on a regular basis.

Why do you need to eat well?

- Because you are what you eat.
- To have more energy.
- To help your body feel good.

How do you eat well?

First, eat mostly nutritious food. The most nutritious foods are those with high fiber, protein and vitamins. These are fruits, vegetables, chicken, fish, eggs, legumes, nuts, etc. Eating nutritious foods gives you the energy necessary to complete each day's tasks and also satisfies your hunger until the next meal. Eating nutritiously will mean reducing your intake of fat, salt and refined sugar. It reduces the risk of cardiovascular diseases, renal diseases, and a lot more. Of course, eating well also excludes the use of illegal substances.

Certainly eating well can cost more and may require you to spend more time cooking, but it's really a good investment in your health and wellbeing. Besides, having roommates during your college years can help you eat better. Here's what my brother Jean, a biology student, said:

> *My roommates and I decided to combine our grocery budgets. Everyone pays a part and it ends up being cheaper for all of us. And the menu is really varied. It can range from spaghetti to salmon to lasagna, etc. We have even eaten lobster and crab!*

In addition, we alternate the cooking responsibility. So the nights you're not the cook, you have extra time to do other things. Also, when you are the cook, you're more motivated to cook a good meal because you're not the only one eating it.

10. Drink Water

Did you know that when you're dehydrated, your mental faculties are reduced? So it is in your best interest to stay well hydrated!

Why do you need to drink plenty of water?

- To help maximize your intellectual faculties.
- To reduce headaches.

How can you be sure to drink enough water?

You need to drink about 2 liters of water every day. To do so, consider carrying a water bottle with you and refill it several times a day.

I also encourage you to avoid energy drinks. They actually reduce your ability to concentrate and affect your sleep and your overall health because they disrupt your hormones.

Of course, I also encourage you to use moderation if you drink alcoholic beverages, even though it can sometimes be tempting to do the opposite, especially at college. If you do drink alcoholic beverages, drink a glass of water between each one to reduce your chances of getting a headache.

A lot of students carry a bottle of water with them all the time. Edith, a graduate student in dental medicine, was one of those. Here's what she says:

> *I drank 4 liters of water each day at college. I carried a big bottle of water and my goal was to refill it several times. Of course, that meant many trips to the bathroom! I was refilling my water bottle during breaks and making a trip*

to the bathroom at the same time. Drinking plenty of water on a daily basis is important. It eliminates toxins. It is also good for your brain. And it reduces hunger cravings! Yeah, you know, hunger cravings: when you're studying and stressed out and want to snack without stopping!

11. Stay Active

Doing physical exercise is extremely important for your life balance, your health and your performance in general.

Why do you need to exercise?

- Because it releases toxins from your body and purifies it.
- Because after you're done, it relaxes you, gives you energy and increases your focus.
- So you can feel good physically and mentally.

How do you need to exercise?

Plan at least 30 minutes of exercise in your schedule every day. Doing your exercise in the morning can be ideal because you get it done before you get distracted by the other activities of the day. Also, going outside every day when it is light is ideal and is especially important in fall and winter. Not only will you breathe fresh air, but being in the sunshine will wake up you more and also reduce the risk of depression.

Commit to it! Your choice of exercise might be to go work out by yourself in the gym, participate in an intramural sport or even just take a quick walk outside. In my case, I like to play badminton so I can see my friends who aren't in any of my classes. I also like to do indoor training in the gym because it gives me the opportunity to empty my mind.

Here is what Edith, the graduate student in dental medicine, says about exercise:

> *Moving every day is extremely important. For example, I exercise in the morning. I think this is the best*

time of day for me because it allows me to have a sense of accomplishment to start my day. And in the morning I'm less distracted by my other responsibilities and by other people. And it's then that I'm more focused.

In college I did CrossFit and cheerleading among other things for exercise. These activities allowed me to meet people and think about something other than my classes. It also allowed me to have fun while doing something good for my body and my mind–because after exercising, I feel good!

12. Get Enough Sleep

This principle means getting the amount of sleep that you need every night.

Why do you need to get plenty of sleep?

- Because while you sleep your brain processes the new knowledge acquired during the day.
- To have plenty of energy each day.
- To purify your body of toxins.
- To avoid spending part of your next day catching up on your sleep.

How do you make sure to get plenty of sleep?

Wake up and go to bed at about the same time every day, including weekends. This helps you establish a routine and you're able to get out of bed more easily in the morning. And don't spend sleepless nights working or studying. If you do, you'll disrupt your sleep cycle and will spend the next few days sleeping and recovering. And this will eventually ruin your health.

Cynthia, a graduate student in psychology, talks about her sleep routine:

> *The most important thing is to have a sleep routine and stick to it. For example, in college I went to bed every night around 10 and got up in the morning around 7. I also tried to do the same on the weekends so I didn't break my sleep routine.*

In addition, get the amount of sleep that you need to perform your best. On average people need to sleep about 7-8 hours a night. Some people need more sleep; others, less. You know how much sleep you need. Also, avoid sleeping more than you need. If you sleep more than you need, you can feel just as tired as if you didn't sleep enough.

Finally, relax for about 30 minutes before going to sleep and, if possible, without any electronics, because most electronic devices are stimulants. Relaxing prior to going to bed will help you clear your mind and prepare your body and mind to sleep, and will help you sleep better. This one change can make a big difference.

13. Schedule a Time to Work and a Time to Play*

Plan your schedule so that each day includes a period of time to work and some time to have fun. They're both important.

Why do you need to plan time to work and to play?

- To make sure that you work at least a little every day.
- To ensure that you free your mind from work and have fun at least a little every day.
- To keep from trying to do both at the same time (multitasking).
- Because you'll be more disciplined to work when it's time.
- Because you'll feel free to have fun when it's time.

In a next principle, we will see that multitasking should be avoided because it reduces your focus and decreases your efficiency.

How do you make time for work and play?

Schedule in your planner at least one period of time for work and one period of time for play every day. Book your time to work first, and schedule it early, during the part of the day when your productivity is maximal. Schedule other periods of time to work during the day if needed. Then, book a time to play, and schedule it during the time of the day when you are the least productive.

And, if you're a person who tends to work without stopping, be sure to give yourself at least a little time each day to play. Here Edith shares with us how she was able to take time for herself during the week as well as on the weekends:

> *When I was in college I worked hard on my coursework all week. But on Friday, it was time to relax. I*

usually found something to do with some friends or with my boyfriend or even by myself. I needed Friday evening to be free time, so I didn't even open a book when I got back from class. It was totally an evening for fun–for watching movies or playing games or whatever.

Then the rest of the weekend, just like the rest of the week, I continued my usual routine. But after about 9 each night, I would stop studying and just enjoy the rest of the evening. I stopped working then because otherwise my brain wouldn't shut down in order for me to be able to fall sleep. After I quit working, I would talk with one of my roommates or talk to my family on Skype or do something else fun or relaxing.

14. Surround Yourself with People Who Encourage You to Grow

This principle means your circle of friends should include a majority of people who will contribute to your growth. Some of these friends will be like you, students who want to succeed and who want to distinguish themselves from others by their involvement in their education. Ideally, you also need to include people who are already more successful than you. Possibly students who have greater responsibility in student organizations or activities.

Why surround yourself with these particular people?

- Because you will become like the people you spend the most time with.
- To have easy access to the advice of successful students and thereby increase your chances of success.
- To create a network of mutually beneficial relationships.

How do you do it?

Surround yourself with energizing, motivating, positive and successful people. Make friends and mentors with these people and learn from them. In contrast, don't hang around with people with low energy who are depressing and negative. Surround yourself with people who want you to succeed, too–people who care about you, such as your close friends and family members.

My brother Jean, a biology student, told me:

It's important to find friends you are comfortable with and can say what you really think.

My roommates are very energizing and have a positive outlook. They are kayak guides. They work outside all day long and get a lot of sun. When they come back to the apartment, they always have a big smile on their face. They are always including me in any activities they plan. It's really nice to have motivated people around me. It helps keep me positive.

In addition, some of my roommates play music. I play the guitar and since they are better than me, I am able to learn a lot from them. It's a great arrangement.

15. Read a Newspaper

This can be a newspaper or an online journal about the world in general or in any specialized field of study. I suggest reading a newspaper instead of watching the news on television because television has too much advertising and includes a lot of information that's not necessarily useful or interesting. And it's easy to get distracted and waste too much time once you start watching television.

Why read a newspaper?

- To stay connected to the outside world.
- To find practical applications of the theories presented in class.
- To discover opportunities and unmet needs in society that you could seize or solve.

How should you read the newspaper?

Choose a newspaper or journal of your choice and read at least the titles and subtitles. For example, it could be the *Wall Street Journal* or *New York Times*. I also encourage you to subscribe to a newspaper or journal in your specialized field of study to keep up with developments in your profession. It is very advantageous for you to keep up with what's going on in your field of study, especially if you want to pursue graduate studies where research is key.

Reading a newspaper is a habit that my brother Jean has adopted. He now reads several newspapers regularly:

> *I try to read more than one newspaper in order to get differing viewpoints. I may read one paper in order to hear*

the views on the left, and another to hear opinions more on the right.

I try to have a balanced view by reading a variety of newspapers. That way I really get a good mix of ideas and opinions.

And reading English newspapers gives me a more global perception than I get reading only French newspapers.

I read a lot during the semester. In fact, I'll often spend my study breaks reading newspapers. It helps give my brain a rest from studying, but at the same time I don't feel guilty for not studying because I'm learning about current events.

Before Classes

The habits that I present here will help you be better prepared for your classes.

16. Understand Your Professors*

Understanding your professors means putting yourself in their shoes and learning to see things from their point of view.

Why do you need to do this?

- To find out how your professors think.
- To understand how they teach their subject.
- To know how they will correct your work and grade your exams.
- To be able to meet their expectations.
- To provide better answers to their exam questions.

How can you understand your professors?

First, realize that most of your professors chose teaching because they are passionate about their subject, want to advance knowledge in their field, and want to transmit that knowledge to students–like you. Also, realize they want you to succeed in their classes. In fact, your professors have worked hard to succeed, to become experts in their field, and to be able to convey this valuable knowledge. And they expect you to work as hard as they did to succeed.

Second, realize that your professors are human and may be, therefore, subjective in their teaching and when grading exams and coursework. Your professors have their own perceptions (preferences and opinions) about the knowledge in their field. For example, they may agree or disagree in part with lecture notes written by another professor, with the material contained in the textbook written by another author, or with a process taught by another professor.

And consciously or not, your professors tend to transmit, in their class, their perceptions of the subject. This can be seen when they are insisting on a point they personally consider most important. And it may be that important to them because they have had significant life experience with the subject. It can also be seen when they are very direct in declaring what they agree or disagree with. Also, consciously or not, they will value exam answers that are more consistent with their perceptions on the subject. For your response to be good, they expect it to be fairly consistent with their perceptions.

Third, realize that it is mainly in the classroom that you will discover the perceptions your professors have on their subject. Think about it. Most teachers didn't write the textbooks that they're having to use. So you can't rely on textbooks written by someone else or lecture notes written by a different professor to be able to understand your professors. It is mainly through listening to them in class that you will learn to understand them and will be able to respond more accurately to their exam questions.

On this topic, Alex, the graduate engineering student, told me:

> *It was the way the professor addressed the formulas in class that indicated whether he just wanted us to be able to properly 'fit' the numbers in the formulas or if he wanted us to know the material well and understand the principles.*

17. Take at Least One Class Outside Your Program of Study

Whatever your field of study, you will probably have to take an elective course to complete the number of credits required to graduate.

Why should you take a course outside your major?

- To think about something different.
- To meet new people.
- To develop new interests.
- To expand your knowledge.

In addition, it can help you to find an application of your knowledge in other areas. Here's what Alex, the mechanical engineering student, explained:

> *By taking courses in other programs, I was able to see how other fields of engineering are thinking. It broadened my knowledge and I realized that there are often similarities between my specific area and other areas of engineering.*
>
> *Although the fields are different, the similarities are there and it makes me think: "My knowledge can also be applied somewhere else!" I started to understand that the knowledge I was acquiring was even more versatile than I originally thought.*
>
> *For example, mechanical engineering and electrical engineering both use differential equations that use the same formulas to solve problems. So while my specialty is mechanical engineering, I understand the concept of*

differential equations and that helps me understand the concepts in electricity.

In short, it allows me to apply what I already know to other areas and understand those areas by analogy. In addition, I understand them more quickly so it reduces my study time!

How do you decide on a course outside your major?

First, investigate the different courses in other majors that might interest you. See what their content and requirements are. Ask the professors or past students about the classes. Finally, decide which one interests you the most. For example, if you are in medicine, it may be a course in business administration. And if you are in elementary education, it could be a course in history.

18. Ask Previous Students about Your Classes and Professors

These students are those who are in the same program as you, but are at least a year ahead of you and have already taken your classes or have already had your professors for a class.

Why do you need to question these students?

- To get any advice they will share about their college experience.
- To help you choose and understand your courses.
- To help you choose and understand your professors.
- To help you better prepare for your exams.
- To guide you in your coursework and class choices.
- To reduce your stress and workload.

How do you go about questioning them?

Question successful students in your program that are at least a year ahead of you. Ask them for information about the classes they recommend, about the workload of certain classes, about the professors they recommend or don't recommend, about the perceptions of your professors about their subject matter, about the type and content of exams and how to study for your exams.

A friend of mine, Marie, shared this about studying kinesiology:

> *In kinesiology, we talked to the students ahead of us in the program about which courses we could take to help us to increase our GPA. We were planning to go into medicine and dentistry so we needed a higher GPA to get into those limited programs.*

They told us, "You should take this course because it's easy to get good grades." Or, "That course has a huge and crazy workload."

That's what I did one semester. I took an easy course that previous students recommended to us. I was able to get higher grades and I was accepted into dental school!

In Marie's case, questioning previous students helped her get higher grades in order to switch to a very limited program.

19. Skim Through Your Course Material*

Your course material includes, among other things, the course syllabus, lecture notes, textbooks and possibly PowerPoint presentations from your professors. These are all documents handed out in class or available online or in a bookstore.

Why should you skim through your material?

- To review the general structure and content of your courses.
- To be better prepared in class.
- To learn more easily in class.
- To figure out what material is not clear after a quick reading so you can be prepared to ask for more in-depth explanations in class.
- To reduce your study time after class in order to understand the material.
- To reduce your workload after class.

How should you skim through the material?

Start by getting the list of lectures notes and mandatory textbooks and go buy them as early as possible. But be careful. You don't always need to buy all the textbooks. I suggest you check with students who've already taken the class.

Once you have your course material, skim through it and familiarize yourself with the general content. Read the table of contents, headings, sub-headings and summaries. If you have more time, consider going through them in more detail. Then, if you think they're relevant, consider doing the recommended readings before your classes. Also consider reading your lectures notes before your class if you have access to them. Some lecture notes may be purchased at the beginning of the semester. Others notes, such as your teacher's PowerPoint presentations, can be accessed online.

And others notes are distributed a few minutes before the beginning of the class.

Edith, a graduate student in physiotherapy and dentistry, told me that she regretted not doing this more:

> *I should have done it more! That's what I learned ... I should have done it more!*
>
> *I found that if I took the time to read my lecture notes for the class, either to arrive a little early before class and just skim through the document that I had just been handed or to take the time to skim the chapter the professor was going to cover in class, I was more alert.*
>
> *And it also helped me better understand where the professor was going in his lecture. There needed to be a series of logical ideas already in my head. That would have been very helpful, but I didn't always do it... and that made it more difficult.*

20. Lighten Your Backpack

This may sound funny, but it's true! Too often students have backpacks that are unnecessarily heavy and bulky.

Why do you need to lighten your backpack?

- To feel lighter and stronger.
- To have more energy.
- To reduce back pain.
- To motivate yourself to carry only essential material.
- To easily store and find your material.
- To save time.

How do you lighten your backpack?

One thing you can do is rent a locker on campus. There are shelves that you can purchase and insert in your locker to create compartments and maximize space. Think about storing your heavy and/or bulky materials there. Consider storing your textbooks in your locker or just leave them at home.

The second thing you can do is just take what you need for that day or that portion of the day. Leave the rest of your materials at home. I suggest using lined paper rather than notebooks to take notes because they are lighter and less bulky. I also suggest you use Duo-Tang notebooks with two internal pockets rather than ring binders. They are also lighter and less bulky. You can easily put your notes inside during the day and transfer them when you get home. But everyone has his own system. Just find one that works for you.

Here's what Cynthia, a psychology graduate student, did with her textbooks:

I had a basket at home with all my books. So I only brought what I needed for the day and that was enough. College textbooks are heavy and bulky. My neurology book must have weighed 20 lbs. by itself!

Also, there were several courses where I didn't buy the books because they were useless. So I only had to carry lecture notes, which were much lighter.

You also might consider using a laptop or tablet to take notes and have your textbooks with you electronically. And I recommend that you carry a small pencil box. Include in it some pens, pencils with retractable lead, highlighters, white-out, a calculator, an eraser and a ruler. And please, don't fill it completely. This little detail can be a source of great frustration when the zipper gets stuck! And I strongly encourage you to prepare your backpack the night before.

During Class

The habits that I suggest here will help you get the most out of your classes.

21. Go to Class

Why do you need to go to class?

- To take your own notes.
- To understand your professor's opinions and views about the subject she teaches.
- To observe the verbal and non-verbal messages of your professor so you'll know what he considers important for your exams and your career.
- To reduce your study time.
- To reduce your workload.

How do you need to attend class?

Attend Class

The most important thing you need to do when you take a course is go to class. In fact, you should always go to class, unless you're seriously ill or have had a death in the family. If for some reason you have to miss, be sure to get the notes from a classmate you trust as soon as possible, make a copy of them, make sure you understand them, getting help from your friend if necessary. Don't hesitate to ask your professor for help understanding the material if you need to.

Be On Time

The second most important thing to do is be on time for class. And the best way to avoid being late is to be a few minutes early. Arriving early also gives you time to skim through the material that will be presented and mentally prepare yourself to learn, which optimizes your learning capabilities.

Here's an experience that Cynthia shares with us:

I always plan to be in class at least 15 minutes early. This has come in handy when the location of my class was changed and I had to go looking for the new location. I also use that time to review the material just before an exam, or when I realize after talking with other students that I forgot to review for the pop test at the beginning of class! That leaves me a little time to review. Hahaha!

And there's nothing more embarrassing than arriving late and disturbing the professor and 200 students who stop listening to him to watch me come in, sit down and get my stuff out of my bag! Even if I try to be quiet, it is IMPOSSIBLE!

Stay Awake

A third important thing is to stay awake in class. If you know you are going to fall asleep, you're better off staying home. Because you'll waste your time and you'll send the message to your professor that what he spends his time teaching you doesn't interest you. In short, it's disrespectful and immature.

22. Pick the Best Seat

The seat that is best for you is not necessarily the best one for other people. Some people prefer to sit in the front row so they have no one except the professor in their field of vision. Others will prefer to sit in the back rows to have a good view of the entire class and be better able to follow any discussion. It's up to you to determine the best location for your learning style.

Why sit in the best seat?

- To reduce noise and visual distractions.
- To increase your focus.
- To maximize your listening.
- To demonstrate your interest.

How do you choose the best seat for you?

Sit at the place that allows you to listen the most carefully to your professor. Ask yourself where's the place where you will clearly and strongly hear your professor's voice. Ask yourself where's the place where you are less distracted. Avoid sitting near any disruptive students–the ones who talk, sleep, chat, text, etc. Instead, sit near conscientious students, the ones who listen carefully, take notes and succeed.

Certainly, the best place to sit depends on each person. For example, here is where the best place is for Cynthia:

> *I always sit at the end of a row in the center of the auditorium. That way, I am facing the center of the board. I also find a seat where I do not have a neighbor directly to my right, since I have a mini bladder. That way I'm not*

bothering anyone when I have to go to the bathroom! Hahaha!

And while it may seem strange at first, I don't sit next to my friends. That helps keep me focused, because the desire to talk to the strangers next to me is much less.

23. Look for Verbal and Nonverbal Messages from Your Professors

Communication consists of verbal and non-verbal aspects. Nonverbal represents most of the communication. So missing out on the non-verbal cues of your professors means you are missing an important part of the message they're transmitting. Another reason why you should go to class!

Why should you be aware of verbal and nonverbal messages?

- To ensure that you receive all the information the professor is trying to transmit to you.
- To extract useful (whether obvious or subtle) information for your exams.

How do you become aware of all the messages your professor is transmitting?

First, listen closely to your professor's voice for signals about the importance of a particular piece of information. It may be a simple variation of the tone of voice or a variation in their speech rate. It may also be the repetition of a word, a concept, an explanation, an example, etc. The amount of time spent explaining a concept can also indicate its importance. These elements are probably essential material that will be included on your exams.

Then, look for gestures and visual signs from your professor indicating the significance of a particular element. One gesture, for example, could be a finger lifted upwardly. There could also be a longer break or introduction before beginning a crucial topic. As for the visual materials, look for anything in bold, underlined or italicized. It could also be signified by an asterisk or another sign of importance.

In my case, I remember that some of our courses in periodontics were taught by graduate students. And those were the easiest courses to study because the graduate students would indicate which material would be included on the exams with a particular image on those PowerPoint slides.

24. Take a Lot of Notes

Why do you need to take notes?

- Because your notes are often more important than your readings.
- To make sure you notice any new material that is not in your readings.
- To be able to skip some or all of your readings.
- Because it is the best way to remember what was covered in class.
- To increase your confidence when studying for exams.

How do you take notes in class?

Most Important Information

First, be sure to take notes on the most important information. This is information:

- the professor emphasizes.
- that responds directly to the course objectives.
- that is the main subject matter of the course.
- that includes details relevant to the course material.

Understand the Meaning

Also, while taking notes, make sure you understand the meaning of the information you're writing down. This will help you avoid unnecessarily writing about something you have already written. It will also help you organize and structure your notes. Also, be sure to write legibly. You want to be able to reread your notes easily and not have to rewrite them.

Write Fast

I suggest you use abbreviations and symbols. This way you'll be able to write faster. Use popular abbreviations and feel free to create your own abbreviations, symbols or designs when you need to repeatedly write the same word or concept. Also, I suggest you write your notes with a pen. It's easier to write and easier to read and it's cleaner than writing with a pencil. You will also get used to writing with a pen, like you'll need to do for most of your exams. Also consider taking your notes on a laptop or tablet. This may be the most appealing option, because you probably type faster than you write.

Use Lined Paper

I suggest you take notes on lined sheets of paper rather than in notebooks, as I explained in a previous principle. Write on the top of the front page the date, your initials, the course title and the topic of the day. I also encourage you to number your pages and staple them together at the end of the class. Your stapled bundles of sheets from each of the different classes of the day will be organized and easy to transport. At the end of the class, indicate on the front page the total number of pages, to help you manage your time better when reading or studying them.

Only Use the Front Side

In addition, I suggest you only write on the front side of each sheet of paper. This will keep the back clean for future additional notes and keep the ink from transferring to the front of the other pages. You may also want to consider staying a few minutes after class to clarify your notes by adding words and symbols or highlighting certain portions while the material is still fresh on your mind. If it helps, consider going over your notes with a friend you trust to be sure they are complete. And if you ever lend your notes, be sure to first make a copy to lend out, so you always have the original.

Adapt to Your Style

The way you take notes must be adapted to your personality. Some people prefer to take notes only on the bare minimum and spend most of the class listening to the professor with their books closed. These people may feel more confident than others about the subject matter, or they may have a better auditory memory, or they may simply learn better this way. Once again, it's up to you to decide the best way for you to take notes, because you know yourself.

But I do think it’s better to take too many notes than not enough. A few times I had classes that didn’t provide lecture notes and didn’t really recommend reference books. In these courses, the only way to remember the material presented in class was to take very detailed notes. And it's easier to be confident during exams when you know that your notes were detailed.

25. Understand the Key Concepts Before Leaving Class

The key concepts are the main ideas, the supporting ideas, and the important details of your courses.

Why do you need to understand the key concepts?

- To save time.
- To reduce your workload.
- To be confident about the material.
- To avoid misunderstanding the information once you get home.

How can you understand the key concepts in class?

Listen carefully, identify these concepts, understand the link between them and ask a question in class, if needed, to clarify anything you don't understand. I recommend you ask a question in class whenever there is an important point that you don't understand. Remember you are paying for the professor to help you learn this material. In addition, most professors are happy to help students, especially when you show interest in the material by asking a question. Remember there is no shame in being confused about a portion of the material. If necessary, consider asking your questions at the end of the class or by visiting the professor during the office hours he makes himself available for students.

Getting clarification from the professor is something many students fail to do. In fact, even after 6 years, Alex has always regretted not following this principle:

> *During one class, the professor explained what a gyroscope is. He brought a big wheel and he showed us how it worked. He explained the rotation and the precise*

movement. He demonstrated and explained all of that to us. But I didn't understand it at all.

I knew how to solve equations. If you gave me a problem and I was told it was a gyroscope, I could easily say what forces were involved and solve the equation. But I didn't understand it.

And I still don't understand it today. That concept is still unclear and it haunts me. Actually it pisses me off! The gyroscope is something really cool and I regret not asking a question in class because six years later I still don't understand it.

After Class

The following habits will allow you to optimize your study time outside of class.

26. Understand Your Course's Syllabus

Why do you need to understand the syllabus?

- Because it contains valuable information to help you study for your exams.
- Because it contains valuable information to help you successfully complete your assignments.
- Because it may warn you about pop tests in your class.

My class on "Dentures" included regular pop tests. And it was only because I had read in the syllabus that there would be pop tests in this class that I was prepared for them.

How can you understand the syllabus?

Know the Course Objectives

First, carefully read the course objectives. They indicate what you must understand and master in order to pass your exams and complete your assignments. They indicate what you need to focus on when you study for your exams. They also indicate the direction that your written or oral assignments should take. In addition to the course objectives, you need to also read the section containing instructions regarding your assignments.

Schedule All Assignments and Exams

Next, find the information about the different tests and assignments. Write in your day planner all the information about each exam: date, time, room, percentage of the final grade, is it cumulative or not. Also write in your daily planner all the pertinent information about each assignment: date due, type of assignment, team or solo, percentage of the final grade, etc.

27. Divide Each Course's Work and Study into Smaller Tasks

Why do you need to divide it?

- To make your tasks more concrete.
- To make your work easier and more motivating to do.
- To reduce the fear and overwhelm associated with the perception of a huge task.

How do you divide your work?

Simply segment your readings, your study time and your long assignments into blocks of work. For example, if you have a research paper to do, break it down into smaller steps: research, outline, draft, editing, and final revision.

For me, it's by dividing my work into concrete tasks that I get motivated to start and to finish my work, especially any assignments that require extensive research.

28. Set Deadlines for Your Tasks

Tasks include study time, readings, short or long assignments, etc.

Why do you need to set deadlines?

- To be sure you complete your work on time.
- To avoid procrastination.
- To reduce your stress.
- To give you the opportunity to reward yourself when you meet your deadline.

How do you set deadlines?

First, determine how much time you'll need to complete each task. Then give each task a reasonable amount of time to be completed. Make sure you give each task a time that is proportional to their importance. And give yourself a deadline to complete each task. Finally, write the deadline date in your daily planner. Then you need to respect your deadlines and reward yourself when you do it!

For example, if you had a research assignment of 10 pages to do, you may assign 5 hours for gathering information, 1 hour for creating the outline, 10 hours for writing the draft and 5 hours for editing and revising. Then you could set aside a number of hours each week to work toward completing each step in order.

Because of these arbitrary deadlines that I set for myself, several of my assignments were completed on time and some even well ahead of the professor's deadline!

29. Start Assignments Immediately

Why do you need to start immediately?

- To begin the process of accomplishing your work.
- To motivate you to continue and finish your work quickly.
- To avoid procrastination.

How do you start?

After segmenting your work into smaller steps, start working on the first step that same week–preferably that same day! In our example of a research paper assignment, the first step may be to find and gather the relevant information.

My friend Cynthia really excels at this. She shared with me this experience that happened to her when working on an assignment as part of a team:

> *In one of my psychology classes, I had to do a 50-page research paper with someone else. And we didn't get to choose our teammates. They were chosen for us. I ended up being paired with a 76-year-old gentleman. He was friendly and very knowledgeable. In fact, he was the student who asked the most questions in class and a lot of times his questions actually lengthened the class.*
>
> *But, when I found out I was paired with him, I was concerned because of his age. I thought, "Will he be able to finish his part by the deadline?"*
>
> *However, I discovered that he was an excellent student, in spite of his age. He was really motivated and we started working on our project the same day that it was assigned–just like I was used to.*

Our project required a lot of research and the presentation had to be given the week after exam week. But we finished our work early, two weeks before the deadline. Most of the other students had not completed their work and ended up working on their research project during the exam week. But we were able to focus on our exams and we both did very well.

30. Read Each Day's Class Notes that Night*

Why do you need to read them that night?

- Because the material is the most recent in your memory.
- Since it's the same day, you'll be able to read them faster and easier.
- Because it will help you remember them longer.
- To save yourself a lot of time trying to recall and understand them later.

How do you read them?

Simply set a time in your schedule each evening to review your notes from that day. And then do it. You'll be surprised at the results. If your time is too limited, at least do an overview of them. An overview will only take a few minutes and will also be effective. Here's what Edith told me:

> *I wasn't always able to read my lecture notes on the same day as class because I was so busy. If I didn't have time to read through them, I skimmed through them quickly. But I made sure I at least did that after every class, especially for my most important classes.*

31. Determine What the Essential Study Material Is

The essential material is the most important and useful material. The rest of the material is less important and not as useful.

Why do you need to make this distinction?

- So you learn only what you need for your exams and your career.
- To avoid wasting your time.
- To reduce your workload.
- To reduce your stress.

How do you determine what's essential?

To distinguish the essential material from the less important material takes critical thinking and self-confidence. It's time to decide what you're going to study, because you can't study everything. This habit is perhaps one of the greatest challenges in this book, but it's one of the most essential. And you can do it! This is the first thing you need to do when you start studying for a new class. Here are a few tips.

<u>Identify Essential Exam Material</u>

First, identify the essential material for your exams. This will include what you're to know in the objectives of the course syllabus. It also includes what your professor highlights in class (by his voice inflection, by repetition, by a gesture or a particular visual indicator, by the amount of time spent on the matter, etc.). It also includes questions the professors ask in class and their answers.

The essential material for exams also includes the material presented in class and in the assigned readings. It usually includes the information contained in the titles and subtitles, keywords found in the required readings. This information is often indicated in bold, italics or underlined. It also includes any graphs, tables, schematics, pictures and any visual aid descriptions.

The essential material is the fundamentals of the course. Answering the following questions can help you determine what is the essential material.

- What is the subject of your course?
- Why is this topic important?
- How does it apply in practice?
- In which context does it apply?
- What are the main elements?
- What support these key elements?
- What are the secondary elements?
- What support these secondary elements?
- What are the relevant details?

Obviously, the relevant material for the exam includes your professor's perceptions about the material. And there's a good chance the same material was essential for this same course last year. So don't hesitate to find students who were successful in this class last year. Ask them about last year's exams–what kind of exams this professor gave.

Identify Essential Career Material

Then identify any additional material that you believe will be essential to your career. It's your job to know what you need to know. It's your job to determine what's necessary for your career.

And then, ignore the other details. In order to do this, you'll have to trust yourself and your judgment.

When I led a study group to study our national board exam in dentistry, this was the most important principle we applied. Marie was part of this group. Here's what she has to say about the experience:

> *We took each of our courses, one after the other, and we looked at the chapter titles and extracted the main ideas, the secondary ideas and any important details. We avoided digging into every single little detail and getting lost. We did study in-depth, but without being perfectionistic about all of the little unnecessary things.*

32. Select Key Material for the Rereading of Your Notes*

This principle involves identifying and reviewing key words or key concepts from your lectures notes each time you read your notes.

Why highlight key material in your notes for rereading?

- To reduce the amount of material you need to read at each reading.
- To extract the most essential material for each reading.
- To highlight the most difficult or less understood material for each reading.
- To become familiar with the material faster.
- To learn the material more quickly and easily.
- To reinforce in your memory the information at each reading.
- To summarize your notes more and more at each reading.
- To ignore the less important or already learned information when you read.

How do you select key material in your notes?

Select Tools and Methods

First, select your tools and determine your methods to highlight the material. Your tools can be highlighters, pens or pencils. Your methods may be to highlight, underline, frame, circle, etc.

Determine Order

Then determine what order you'll use your tools and methods for each rereading. For example, the order might be to highlight with one color, then another, then underline, then frame, etc.

First Rereading

So during your first rereading, select the most important information with the method and the tool of your choice. For example, this first selection can be done by highlighting.

Second Rereading

Then, during your second rereading, highlight (from the information you selected in your first rereading) the information that you consider more important. This second selection can be done with a different color highlighter than the first selection.

Subsequent Rereadings

And do the same for all your subsequent rereadings. Use a new tool or a new method each time. This will allow you to distinguish each of your selections. Ideally, use at the beginning lighter colored tools, and continue with darker and more pronounced colored tools. This will allow you to recognize your latest selection.

By following these tips, you'll soon find that at each of your rereadings, the material that you have to read constantly decreases and the material that you remember increases!

Reread Weekly

Go through this "selective" reading of your notes for each class every week. Each rereading will take you less and less time. And you'll be surprised when you see that you only have a few words per page to read the night before your exam and that you already know it! This method of rereading your material has benefits you'll appreciate through your education.

If/When to Transcribe

Finally, I recommend you not transcribe all your notes as you read them, because there are just too many. If you try to transcribe them all, you probably won't have time to do it and that will leave you even less time to reread–which is the benefit you're trying to attain–not perfect-looking notes and not trying to remember every single word of your notes.

But if you're the type learned who needs to transcribe information in order to remember it, I suggest you wait until you've done some rereading and have selected the essential material and reduced your reading. Then transcribe those selections, because they will contain only the really essential and relevant material that you need to remember.

33. Select Key Material for the Rereading of Your Assigned Readings

This is the same principle as the previous one, but this time it applies to your assigned readings. These readings are the textbook chapters, articles and other documents that your professor assigns for reading either in class or on the syllabus.

Why select the key material from your assigned readings for rereading?

- For the same reasons given in the previous principle.
- Because you probably won't have enough time to do a full rereading.

How do you select the key material?

Use the same method as the previous principle.

I've known students who were afraid to mark in their textbooks because they were planning to sell them at the end of the class. But people and bookstores will purchase used, well-marked textbooks. So don't be afraid to follow the steps I shared in the previous principle.

If you want to learn effectively, you need to handle the material, own the material and leave your marks in your books. Highlighting and marking your documents helps you learn and will give you a great advantage in the long run. And the benefits you enjoy are greater than the gain you will realize by selling an unmarked textbook.

For me, the best way to select the information that applied to me was with highlighters. I highlighted with different colors, from paler ones to darker ones, every time. I would start with the yellow highlighter, then orange, then pink, then blue, and then continued by underlining and circling the information. I call this the "progressive selection." I used it in most of my classes. It was an incredible feeling to only have to read a few last keywords the day before the exam and feel confident and prepared to take the exam!

34. Decide If Your Reading Assignments are Worth Your Time*

Your reading assignments include the information you have to read in order to pass your exams. Your reading assignments also include any reference material that allows you to gather information you need in order to complete a long assignment, to search for an answer to a specific question, etc. Your readings–mandatory, optional or voluntary–are worth your time only if they help you meet your goals. If they don't help you meet your goals, don't read them, because that would be a big waste of your time.

One important thing to know about any reading assignment is the 80/20 rule, taught by Paul R. Scheele in his book titled *Photoreading: Read with greater speed, comprehension, and enjoyment to absorb complete books in minutes.* This rule says that about 80% of the relevant information is usually found in 20% of the total text.[2] So, if you're smart, you won't waste your time reading 100% of the text to get the 80% of relevant information. Instead, you will learn to find the 20% of the text where 80% of the relevant information is located. By learning to do this, you will avoid reading the irrelevant information and you'll get directly to the point.

Why do you need to figure out which of your reading assignments should be read?

- Because all the reading assignments aren't necessary.
- To avoid wasting your time doing unnecessary reading.
- To reduce your workload.
- Because you can be successful on many of your exams by only using your detailed lectures notes. (This is where the advantage of taking lots of notes comes into play!)

How do you discern which reading assignments you need to read?

First, determine what the purpose of your reading assignment is.

- Do you need to look for new relevant information to help you prepare for your exams?
- Do you need to look for precise information to help you understand a particular part of the study material?
- Do you need to find relevant information to answer an assigned question?
- Do you need to summarize your reading?

Second, skim quickly through your reading, flipping through the pages. When you skim, consider these three things.

1. Consider the time and workload that a reading assignment requires, whole or partial.
2. Consider the time you have available to read.
3. Most importantly, consider what new relevant information, different from what you already have, you could extract to fulfill your purpose for this reading assignment.

Take the most popular case where you read to find relevant information you need to study for exams. In this situation, you should ask yourself two things.

1. What is the relevant information, different from what's in your notes, that you may extract?
2. Would studying your notes alone be sufficient to meet your goals for this class?

To figure out if your notes are enough, ask yourself the following questions.

- What has been your past experience with this professor?
- What experience did the students have last year?
- Do your notes contain all the answers to the class objectives? If so, your notes are sufficient to help you make a good grade on your exams and you can skip your reading assignment.

Finally, ask yourself if doing your readings will really benefit you and if taking the time to read it is a good use of your time. If they will not really benefit you and will not give you new relevant information, ignore them. Obviously, in this process, you need to use your better judgment and then trust yourself to know what's best.

This is another principle that Cynthia applied:

During my first two years in college, I bought all the extra reference books and it cost me a boatload of money.

I also did all the recommended readings. Then my professors told me at the end of the course: "Everything on the exam has been covered in class. The readings are not under consideration." From that moment on, I never did any extra reading assignments. And I did well in all my classes.

I felt this was a wise decision for me, because in those earlier times, when I did the readings, I couldn't even remember them when it came time for the exam! I remember a time when I needed to remember a specific piece of information that was in one of my readings. I knew that it was in a small box at the bottom of the left page, but I couldn't recall it.

I realized that if I didn't have the time to reread my reading assignments enough to remember them, there was no need to read them. And I sure didn't have time to reread everything the night before the exam. That's impossible.

35. Do Your Readings in a Way that Serves Your Purpose

Obviously, this is talking about the reading assignments that you have determined are worthy of your time.

Why read with a method that best meets your goal?

- To read only the relevant information you need (remember the 80/20 rule).
- To reduce your reading time.
- To reduce your workload.

How do you determine which reading method is best?

<u>Is a Partial Reading Enough?</u>

First, determine if a partial reading is sufficient to meet your goal. Your goal can be to read to prepare for exams, to clarify a specific point of the study material, to search information for an assignment, to make a summary, etc. And if a partial reading is sufficient to meet your goal, then that's all you need to do! Save yourself from doing a full read. The good news is that in most cases, a partial reading is sufficient.

<u>To Prepare for Exams</u>

For example, say you're reading to find new relevant information to prepare you for your exams. To know if a partial reading is sufficient, ask yourself the following questions.

- What is your experience with this professor?
- What experience did previous students have with this professor?

- Can you meet your goals for this class by reading only the relevant material? The answer to this last question is often "yes" because of the 80/20 rule.

How do you find new relevant information for you to study for your exams? Search for new important information in the table of contents, titles and subtitles, in introductions and conclusions, in explanations under pictures, tables or graphs, and in summaries at the end of sections or chapters. When you find something new, spend your time reading where the text elaborates on this subject.

Two More Uses

Let's look at two other cases where a partial reading is also sufficient.

- When you're reading to help you understand a particular part of the study material, search for the keyword in the glossary and go directly to the relevant pages.
- When you're reading to find information to answer the main question of an assignment, read the table of contents, headings and sub-headings. Plus, read the glossary, looking for relevant keywords and go directly to the relevant pages.

For scientific articles, consider the following approach used by Jean, a biology student:

> *For scientific articles, I just read the title and the abstract. If it does not appeal me, I don't read the article. If it appeals me, I go directly to the discussion and conclusion.*

Summarizing Your Reading

Here's another case where a partial reading is enough: when you read to make a summary of your reading. In this case, read the table of contents, headings and sub-headings. Read introductions and conclusions. Read the first and last sentences of paragraphs. Read summaries at the end of chapter and read the explanations under images, tables or graphs.

Ask Previous Students

However, if a partial reading is not sufficient to meet your goal, consider fully reading your reading assignments. And consider asking previous students about the relevance of the reading assignments for exams, to help you know whether they are worth your time.

36. Understand the General Content of Your Classes*

This principle should be applied before memorizing any study material.

Why do you need to understand the outline of your class?

- To understand the main principles of your class.
- To understand the relevance of what you memorize.
- So the memorization that you do will have context and make sense.
- So the memorization can be done more easily.
- To avoid memorizing something that is logical.
- To avoid memorizing unnecessary parts of the material.
- To avoid wasting your time.

This principle was very important for Edith's "Diagnosis" class in dentistry. Here is what she shares:

> *The first thing I needed to know for my diagnosis class was to understand what would appear white and what would appear black on x-rays. If I already understood this principle, that would help me determine what I was looking at on an x-ray.*
>
> *After that, I needed to understand why the lesions were white or black, and how they may evolve. Are they going to be pitted? Are they going to be attached to something or not?*
>
> *So it was necessary for me to understand these different elements and their links with diseases before memorizing their characteristics. Otherwise, I would not have understood what I memorized.*

How do you understand the outline of your class?

First, identify the main and secondary ideas of your class and all relevant details. This information can be found mainly in your notes, in your assigned readings and in the presentations shared by your professor.

For your notes, use the latest selection made during your last rereading of your notes (remember principle 32: "Select Key Material for the Rereading of Your Notes"). For your assigned readings, use the table of contents, headings, sub-headings and all relevant details. Then, on your professor's presentations, use their presentation outline, titles, subtitles and relevant details.

Finally, look and be sure you understand the link that unites the main and secondary ideas and the important details together.

37. Escape to a Secret Location Every Week*

This secret location should be a quiet place where you are alone–not the campus, your workplace, or your home. This is a place other than where you spend the majority of your time.

Why do you need to escape to such a place?

- To temporarily disengage from the student world.
- To relax and rejuvenate.
- To come back a stronger and more energized student.
- To reduce your stress.
- To help you maintain a balanced life.
- To free your mind of its concerns and make room for new ideas. (It is often when you are not at work or at school that you have genius ideas about your work or school!)

How do you escape to a secret location?

Get off of the physical college campus, away from your workplace and away from your home. Go and spend time outdoors in a quiet and rejuvenating place. It can be walking in the park, walking in the woods, walking on the waterfront, walking in a residential area in the early morning, etc.

This is something my friend Cynthia did almost every day. Here's what she has to say about it:

> *I have a pony called Mistral. Every day while I was in college I went to visit him in the stables where he was living. I cleaned his box, brushed him, took rides with him and spent time there simply sitting around doing nothing.*

Going to the stables allowed me to shut my brain off and just do something manual, without any intellectual effort. It allowed me to have a balanced life.

38. Study in Blocks of 50 Minutes

Why study in blocks of time?

- To give you a short break between long periods of study.
- To keep you from getting burned out from studying.
- To increase your focus.
- To help you study efficiently.

How do you break up your study periods?

Discipline yourself to take a break after 50 minutes of study. Remind yourself that it's good for you and that it helps you study more efficiently! Then leave wherever you're studying and change your mindset for 10 minutes. Go for a walk, go outside and get some fresh air, go grab a snack, etc.

The goal of this principle is to take regular breaks when you're studying intensely. It is a concept Edith followed:

> *I studied by blocks of time, by chapter, or by module. And I took frequent breaks. I spent time reading and then I would tell myself, for example, that after studying this chapter, I would take a break. I would spend some time on the internet or I would stand up and do some stretches. But I did something different and then I came back.*
>
> *When I stopped studying, I stopped thinking about the subject. I would go talk to my roommate or I would go to the gym. I also made some goals. For example, I told myself, "OK, I will study hard until 8pm because that's when my favorite TV show comes on." That gave me motivation.*
>
> *I did the same thing when I was planning to go to the gym. "OK, I'll study this chapter until 8pm because then I'll go to the gym." After my workout, I came back and it was*

nice because my brain wasn't working overtime when I was trying to go to sleep.

I set those particular goals for myself because they worked for me: I like to watch my favorite television show and I like to go to the gym.

39. Plan Each Week's Schedule on Sunday Night

Why plan your week?

- To remind yourself of the tasks you need to accomplish.
- To reserve a period of time in your schedule to accomplish them.
- To be sure you achieve the top priority tasks first.
- To complete the work from the previous week that hasn't been done yet.
- To make sure you keep your activities and work focused so you can meet your goals.
- To begin your week with confidence.
- To reduce your stress.

How do you plan your week?

Determine what tasks you need to accomplish in the next week: classes, work, study, activities, postponed obligations of previous week, etc. Then schedule, if it is not already done, a time in your schedule to achieve each one of them. Finally, make sure to keep track of all your tasks for the following Sunday.

This system worked great for me. I took about 10 to 15 minutes every Sunday and planned a time in my schedule for everything I needed to get done. Most of the time, I managed to accomplish it all. And if I didn't get to complete a task, I made it a priority for the next week, based on its importance. My stress was reduced and it motivated me a lot, because I couldn't wait to start my week to accomplish what I had scheduled.

Before Exams

The following habits will help you to maximize your preparation for your exams.

40. Anticipate What Will Be on Your Exam*

Why do you need to anticipate the material that will be on your exam?

- To help you know what to study.
- To reduce your study time.
- To give you confidence.
- To reduce your stress.

How do you figure out what will be on your exam?

1. Determine what material your professor has emphasized in class–either by what he expressed verbally or non-verbally. This means you need to go to class, go to review sessions, and pay attention to the questions asked in class. The material presented in class will certainly be found on your exams. It's not certain the additional information contained in the reading assignments will be included on the exams.

2. Reread the class objectives in the syllabus. The exam questions usually contain questions that ask you to prove that you understand the class objectives. What the class objectives state you need to know and understand will be found on your exams. Find out whether your exam is cumulative or not. If it is cumulative, it will include all material covered since the beginning of the semester.

3. Determine the expectations of your professor. Ask yourself if your professor expects you to recite the material from memory. That type of professor typically gives few examples and explanations in class. He usually focuses on facts, theories, characteristics, enumerations (the "what" of the material). If that is the case, your exam may contain mainly memorization and comprehension questions.

Then ask yourself if your professor expects you to understand the material. This type of professor typically gives lots of examples and explanations. He usually emphasizes the logic (the "how" of the material) and the reason (the "why" of the material) of things. If that is the case, you may have mainly comprehension questions on your exam.

4. Determine your professor's views of the material. Ask yourself these questions.

- Does he have the same view as the author in the readings or is his view different?
- What is his view?
- What is his opinion about the subject he teaches?
- How does he justify his opinion?
- What material does he believe is most important?
- Why?

And remember: the right answers to exam questions are often those that are consistent with your professor's views toward the material.

5. Ask previous students what kinds of questions your professor asked them: comprehension questions, memorization questions, multiple-choice, etc. Ask them if he asked any kind of trick questions. Ask them if material from the assigned readings was included on the exams. As I stated before, you can earn a good grade on a lot of tests using only your own detailed notes.

6. See if there are any old exams available. And if so, practice using them. There is a good chance that these types of questions will be similar to the ones on your next exam.

Depending on the class, the old exams can be a real gold mine. Alex tells us about his experience:

Our course on thermal mechanics was really difficult. The professor was very knowledgeable in his field. On the exams, he asked the most detailed questions ever. And there were lots of them on his exams. It was impossible to do well on his exams, unless you had superhuman qualities. But his exam questions were the same type every year.

So if I had the exam questions from the past 10 years, I had my next exam somewhere in there. Those who didn't use the old exam questions to study got an average grade of 30%, while those who used them got an average grade of 80%.

I got the old exam questions from previous students as well as those on file at the student association.

41. Study in the Way that Works Best for You

This principle is consistent with the one at the beginning of the book that encourages you to discover who you are and to know what factors influence your productivity.

Why study in the way that works best for you?

- To reduce your study time.
- To associate "study" with "efficiency."
- To be satisfied that you know the material.
- To increase your confidence.

How do you study in a way that works best for you?

1. Study in places where it is easy for you to focus. These are the places where distractions are reduced–like the library, an empty classroom, or any other empty room, etc. I suggest you avoid studying in your room because that's where the distractions abound! I encourage you to change where you study a few times. This will allow you a change of scenery, help you avoid boredom, and it will also strengthen your memory by creating associations between your study location and your study material.

This is what Cynthia shares with us about how places influenced her focus:

> *In terms of places to study, the stable has been a total failure. Hahaha! I was always bothered by my pony who kept sticking his nose in my books, not to mention muddy clothes that wouldn't come clean. And even though I was isolated, I was still getting up to see what my pony was doing. So I determined I have zero focus at the stables because there's always something much more interesting to do!*

At home, it's a little better. But again, it seems to me that once I'm sitting in front of my books, suddenly getting on the internet, watching TV or even cleaning the house seems much more appealing! Not to mention the box of cookies that talks to me from the pantry or the cat coming over and lying on my opened book.

So for me the best place to study was on campus, because I have nothing else to do there and nothing else grabbing my attention there. So on campus my studying goes much faster because I'm focused. And since I finish faster, I have more free time for my hobbies.

2. Study during times of the day when your efficiency is maximized. Of course, you know yourself. Is it early in the morning? During the day? In the evening? In any case, it is certainly not overnight!

Cynthia knows her most effective time of the day:

The moment I am the most productive to study is in the morning after breakfast and after a good night's sleep. In the afternoon, I have absolutely no motivation and at night it's even worse, since my brain switches off from studying after two minutes!

3. Study during the time of the semester when you are less in a rush. Usually it's early in the semester. That is the ideal time because you have more time. You are calmer and less stressed. You are more receptive to learning. So take this time to skim through the material of your upcoming classes. And perform an initial review of your assigned readings, if you think they are worth it.

4. Be sure you're in the right mindset when you study. First, motivate yourself to study before you start your study time. This will help you associate "study" with "motivation" and avoid burnout from

studying. Then remind yourself of past successes in order to boost your self-confidence and optimize your learning capabilities. Finally, do not study when you're losing interest or are burned out. In fact, when you feel that your brain has switched off from your study material, take a break or find a way to motivate yourself to study!

5. Take care of your body and your health. Dress comfortably when you study. Eat light and nutritious meals to maximize your energy. Avoid studying when you are exhausted because you would be wasting your time–you'll either burn yourself out or make yourself sick. When you're exhausted, rest and reenergize.

6. Analyze your past personal experiences where you studied effectively and those where you were less effective. Then try replicating your past productive experiences and avoid repeating your past unproductive experiences.

42. Memorize Early, Regularly and Effectively

Some of your classes are more focused on comprehension, others on memorization. In the context of comprehension, if you understand the material, you may skip the memorization of the material. In a context of memorization, in addition to understanding the material, you'll need to memorize it.

Generally, however, I suggest you memorize what you understand. It is one thing to understand the logic that unites various elements together (comprehension). But it is another thing to remember all these different elements without help or reminders (memorization). In addition, it is after you understand the outline of the material that you can start memorizing it.

Why memorize *early*?

- Because the sooner that you start memorizing, the sooner you're done memorizing, and the faster you can review what you have memorized and the faster you can reinforce the material in your memory.

Why memorize *effectively*?

- To reduce your study time.
- To reduce your workload.

Why memorize *regularly*?

- Because by regularly reviewing what you've memorized, the memorized material is imprinted more strongly into your memory and you will remember it more easily and for a longer period of time.
- To increase your confidence about the subject.

- To reduce your workload during exams week.
- To reduce your study time during exams week.
- To reduce your stress.
- To strengthen the general knowledge needed for your career.

How do you memorize *early*?

Start memorizing from the first week of class.

How do you memorize *effectively*?

Most Important First

Start by memorizing material from the most important or the most complex class. First memorize the most important material. This is the material that represents the content of the exam that you anticipate (remember principle 40: "Anticipate What Will Be On Your Exam"). And memorize first the information that you remember the least.

Create Associations

Then create associations between different elements of a concept and your life experience. Use memories of your daily life to strengthen your memory: people, events, songs, work, activities, words, etc. And connect it to senses to reinforce your memory: sight, touch, smell, hearing, etc.

Also create associations between different elements of a concept and a real or fictitious picture. Use your imagination. The only limit is the one you impose. Again connect it to senses: sight, touch, smell, hearing, etc. And connect to it humor if you can. The more absurd or funny, the more you remember it.

Mnemonic Tricks

Then create mnemonic tricks to help you remember, in a single word or phrase, the various elements related to a concept. These tricks should make sense to you. But it is not necessary that they make sense to anyone else. Also, do something more than just reading passively. Write, sing, move, draw, gesticulate, say aloud, etc. It will create even more associations with your study material.

Various Communication Methods

Also, use multiple ways of communication to memorize the material. This will strengthen your memory even more. For example, read it. Then write it down (do not recopy all your notes, however, only keywords). Writing the material can take various forms: note, drawings, marks, highlighting, etc. Then say it, either to yourself or when in study groups. Listen to it when others say it in study group.

Use Your Intelligence Types

Also, take advantage of your different types of intelligence when memorizing. You must get to know yourself and find the study techniques that suit you best. This is not necessarily doing things like everybody else, but doing things that work for you so you optimize your study efforts. If you are visual, you may learn best by seeing things, writing summaries, drawing pictures and diagrams, as well as using color.

If you are kinesthetic, you may learn best when you study by moving and using your hands and your body. If you have a musical intelligence, you may learn best when listening to music while studying and perhaps even creating songs and rhythms. Then, if you have a social intelligence, you may learn best by interacting with others in a study group and explaining the material to others.

Otherwise, if you have a reflective intelligence, you probably learn best by studying alone and in a quiet place. If you have a logical intelligence, you probably learn best by using numbers and creating links between elements of the material. And if you have a linguistic intelligence, you may learn best by using words in different ways, either by reading, writing or explaining the material to others.

Be Student and Professor

Also, consider explaining the material to yourself as if you were both the student and the professor. And consider explaining your knowledge of the material to other students, as in study groups. This strengthens and deepens your knowledge of the material. Also consider sharing the content of the material you are memorizing with a successful classmate so that you can see if what you're memorizing fits and to increase your confidence in your knowledge of the material.

Review the Logic

Finally, remember that in a context where the material is logical, you may not have to actually memorize each step, since you'll probably already know them because of the thread that ties these steps together. So, you just have to review this logic often enough to keep remembering it. Also note that when you lack time, it is best to memorize the material presented in class at the expense of the readings.

How do you memorize ***regularly***?

Review the key material of your classes each week (that you selected during your last rereading–remember principle 32: "Select Key Material for the Rereading of Your Notes"), then try to remember it without looking at it. Note that every time you see the information again, it will take you less time and you'll remember more and more, and you'll probably realize, even before the night before the exam, that you already know it all.

Every weekend while I was in college, I used to review my important notes for each class and the mnemonics I had created. By the time midterms were over, I had been through my notes and stuff about 7-8 times. So by then I was already almost ready for my exams!

43. Consider Using a Study Group

Why use a study group?

- To review the study material from different perspectives.
- To evaluate the strength of your knowledge of the material.
- To reinforce your knowledge of the material.
- To have a more balanced knowledge.
- To help your classmates.
- Because studying with others can be very motivating.

How do you use a study group?

1. Determine if study groups are for you. Ask yourself:

- What are your experiences with study groups with good classmates?
- Does it match your personality?
- Does it benefit you?

Also understand that the person who best masters the material can find that she wastes her time in study groups. If this is the case, she should avoid using study groups. On the other hand, if she considers it as an opportunity to enhance her knowledge - which should be the case - then study groups are appropriate.

2. Find the right teammates. If you don't find student who are serious about the study group, I suggest you avoid study groups because you'll lose your energy and waste your time. Good teammates are those that have the following characteristics: help each other, they know you and you know them, they attend group meetings and are disciplined, are punctual to the meetings, are respectful, have the same goal as you–to succeed, are ideally as

intelligent as you (or even more intelligent) and can agree on the guidelines for your study group. Usually, these are your true friends.

3. Determine what is the best way for you to study in groups.

- Is it having a mentor in the group explaining the material to others?
- Is it to be the tutor?
- Is it listening to the tutor speaking, following with your notes and asking questions?
- Or is each of you explaining the material, one teammate after the other?

4. Create a team of up to 3-4 teammates. With more than that, there is less discipline and you're more likely to waste your time. A study group does not always need a tutor. But if you prefer to have one, choose among yourselves the one who knows the material best, who is capable of guiding the study group and who ensures that the study group is productive.

5. Establish all the conditions about your group meetings: study schedule, location, time, duration, etc. Also, each of you should commit to having done individual study and understanding the outline of the material prior to studying together. This way, the study group will be more effective. If your teammates are not prepared, they will make unnecessarily repetitions of the material and will waste the time of others who are more prepared.

In addition, I suggest that you plan to stop meeting a few days before the exam. I also suggest taking short breaks of about 10 minutes after each 50 minutes of study, to clear your mind and reenergize you. I recommend you keep an eye on the time (with your phone, clock, watch, etc.) to make sure you cover all the material you have planned to study.

6. Avoid focusing too long on one concept. The study should advance and avoid neglecting other concepts. Even when there is only one person who does not understand after several explanations, go to the next concept. You must prioritize group productivity over than individual productivity. And each of you should plan to complete your study individually as needed after the meetings.

7. Seek to manipulate the material in different ways. It may be by repeating the material, explaining, asking questions to others on what might be found on the exam, asking tricky questions, listening to explanations of others and considering new perspectives to handle the material, formulating answers to others' questions, etc.

8. Choose a quiet study place and consider changing your study group location a few times. You could meet at the library, in a classroom, in an empty room, in a quiet cafe, etc. Occasionally changing the location will help you prevent boredom and enhance your knowledge by making associations between your study locations and your study material.

Study groups can be very advantageous when you find the right teammates. This is the case of Marie. She shares her experience with study groups:

> *Study groups are practical. They allowed me to reduce my stress because I could validate my studying, whether I was moving in the right direction or wrong direction or even studying too deep. Each teammate was able to bring something valuable.*
>
> *In addition, we were lucky because we had a genius on our team!*
>
> *And add to that, hearing someone explain the material when someone doesn't understand it and explaining it again to others when my turn comes, allowed me to*

comprehend the material. And after that, I didn't need to study it any further. So it greatly reduced my study time.

44. Review Your Key Material the Day Before and the Morning of the Exam

Reviewing the material means a brief overview of the material, not in-depth studying or intense memorization at the last minute.

Why do you need to review it?

- So that the study material will be very fresh in your mind.
- To give you confidence.
- Because you will not need to do more than review if you study the material every week.

How do you review?

Review the latest selection of your notes, and your readings, if applicable. Review the last selected keywords. Also review your key mnemonics, acronyms and associations. Obviously, avoid reviewing all your notes and all your readings. You won't have time and it will cause you to panic.

And if reviewing until the last minute stresses you, consider doing what Alex did:

> *I reviewed the key material the morning before the exam, but not up until the last minute. I stopped reviewing at least one hour before the exam so I wouldn't be stressed.*

45. Reduce Your Stress Before Your Exam

Why do you need to reduce your stress?

- To be more relaxed.
- To be more confident.
- To be more focused.
- To keep your nerves under control.

How do you reduce your stress?

The Day Before

The day before, prepare all the necessary allowed materials for your exam: pens, white-out, bottle of water, watch (you probably can't take your cell phone), etc. Get a good night's sleep. Do not study at night at the expense of sleep. And consider using two alarm clocks so you won't worry about being sure you get up on time. Have a nutritious breakfast.

The Morning Of

The morning of the exam, do an overview of only the most essential material, and just for a few minutes Also, give yourself extra time to travel to your exam location. This will help you in case something unexpected happens, so you can avoid arriving late, and so you can pick your choice seat if seats are not assigned.

Right Before Exam

Consider avoiding any discussions about the study material with other students a few minutes before your exam. No student has studied exactly the same for the exam. Some have studied things that others have not studied and vice versa. If you start discussing the material with others, you can easily get stressed and lose your confidence.

However, understand that this is also a case-by-case basis. If you know that you will stay confident even when discussing the exam with others, chatting with them may help you remember some forgotten details. So these last minute discussions could be useful. But if you don't feel so confident, it's better to avoid these discussions so you won't panic.

This was the case of Marie, who preferred to avoid discussions right before exams:

> *I tried as much as possible to avoid other students and not to listen to discussions about the exam or particular study material other people studied. There are always students who know more than you do and that was stressful to me.*
>
> *The few minutes before the exam, I tried to clear my head and think of something else. And while I was doing the exam, I was calm and not stressed.*

Students to Avoid

Also, stay away from students who ask you questions about the material at the last minute. Some of them are stressed and can stress you out! To protect your peace of mind and confidence, avoid being around theses students right before your exam. Protect your confidence.

Use the Restroom and Breathe

I also encourage you to go to the bathroom before the exam, even if you have no need to at the moment. Sometimes exams can last up to three hours. And often you can't leave your exam room until your exam is done. Also, consider taking deep, slow, controlled breaths in the few minutes before your exam. It will help you control your nerves and relax.

Visualize Success!

Finally, I strongly encourage you to visualize while you wait that you ace your exam. Visualize that you know all the answers to the questions and that you make an extremely high grade.

During Exams

The following habits will help you do your personal best on your exams and class assignments.

46. Skim Through Your Exam

Once you receive your exam, give it a quick overview.

Why do you need to do an overview of the exam before you begin?

- To be sure you allow a reasonable amount of time to answer each question.
- To be sure you answer all the questions in the time allotted for the test.

How do you skim through your exam?

Start by flipping through the pages of your exam. Notice the number of pages. Then notice where the long questions are. Also notice if there are any questions on the back of the pages so you don't neglect to answer them.

Then, plan approximately how much time you can spend on each page. You will, of course, need to know what time your exam ends.

Finally, be sure you allow some time to review your answers before you turn in your exam.

Skimming through your exam is a habit that a lot of upperclassmen have learned is very beneficial. Here's what Edith has to say about this habit:

> *I learned that as soon as I received my exam, I needed to look at how many questions there were, the type of questions included, and how many pages there were. This gave me an idea of the amount of time I would need to complete the exam. And I always tried to allow a little time at*

the end to review my answers and to be sure I didn't forget to include my name and other required information.

47. Use Good Test-Taking Strategies*

A careless and/or repeated error on your exam can cost you a lot of points unnecessarily. To prevent this from happening, use good test-taking strategies during your exams.

Why do you need to have a strategy to take a test?

- To increase your chances of getting the right answers.
- To increase your chances of getting a good grade.

How can you take an exam using good strategies?

1. Read all the instructions beginning on the very first page to avoid making a costly mistake. This is very important because you may be asked, for example, to respond only to two out of the four questions. If necessary, reread the instructions to be sure you understand them.

2. Highlight the tasks requested in the question. Look for the topic of the question. And look for verbs that require you to develop a specific response: define, describe, explain, demonstrate, apply, combine, analyze, evaluate, create, etc.

3. Make sure you understand the question before you begin answering it. If you don't understand a question after some rereading or you don't know the answer, skip it and keep moving. Simply responding to other questions can give you an idea of what the previous answer may be or what the question is asking. When the answer finally comes, write it down immediately so you don't forget it.

4. Allow more time for questions that are worth more points. In some cases, these may be longer questions. In other cases, they

could be shorter questions. Also be sure to prioritize the questions that are worth more points if you're running out of time.

5. Write neatly and legibly. Usually, you write with a pen. If you use abbreviations, make sure they are generally accepted. Remember that your professor needs to be able to read and correct your writing.

6. Be concise and limit yourself to the essential subject when answering short answer questions. Notice the space allowed or the number of lines provided. This indicates the expected length of your answer. Some professors will penalize you when your answer exceeds that suggested length.

7. Use this strategy to answer multiple-choice questions. First, read the question. Then answer the question in your head without looking at the choices provided. This will help you avoid being biased by the choices. Then read the provided answer choices in order and consider them all one after the other by either retaining or eliminating them. Select the one that best answers the question.

Mark your multiple-choice responses on the answer sheet as you finalize each answer. This may not be in order, so be sure to indicate your answers on the answer sheet at the appropriate place and for the right question. When two opposite answer choices are presented among the choices, often one of them is wrong while the other is right. And when "always," "never" or "only" is used, it generalizes the statement and is often the wrong choice.

8. Use this strategy to answer essay questions. First, read the question. Then, highlight the important elements that are being asked. Then, think about your answer and brainstorm. Next, make a plan where you have some space to write (on the back of the page, in the margin, etc.). Then write your answer in a logical and organized manner. Respond using several paragraphs: one for introduction,

some for development and one for conclusion. Use a paragraph for each idea. Also, use all the available space for your answer, but avoid exceeding it. Again, some professors penalize when you exceed the allotted space.

9. Avoid any traps. Watch out for words that generalize a statement such as "always," "never," "all," "none," etc. Also pay attention to the words that change a question, such as "except," "unless," "all are false except," "all are true except," etc. Also pay careful attention to the units of measurement. For example, make sure you read "mg" instead of "g." And be on the lookout for words that are similar to other words.

10. Be well prepared for any open book exams. These are often the most difficult exams to take. They require not only a good understanding of the material, but you also have to know where to find information easily in your notes. That is why during your preparation for the exam, you must organize your documents so you can quickly find what you are looking for. Usually in this type of exam, you will find that your answers require a lot of development.

11. Know how to find an answer to a question when you weren't able to answer it the first time through the exam. There are at least four ways to try to answer it. One is to look at the other questions or the multiple-choice answers to see if it can be found somewhere else on the exam. This is often the case for multiple-choice questions, where one of the answer choices of a question may be part of the answer to a question somewhere else on the exam.

A second way is to use your knowledge of your other classes, your life experiences and your work experience. A third way is to consider if there is another way to adequately approach answering the question. Then, a fourth way is to ask yourself: if you were the professor, what would your answer be?

12. Consider answering the questions in order, or possibly in a different order. It depends on the situation.

Here is what Edith said about it:

> *When I took an exam, if there were any essay questions, I sometimes started with those because they were typically worth more points. And then I would finish with the multiple-choice questions because those were easier.*
>
> *But my decision on the order was also based on the type of exam it was and the type of professor I had. Sometimes it was better to start with the multiple-choice questions because the answer choices might contain some keywords and elements I could use to answer other questions. Then I would use those keywords when I did the essay questions.*

13. Review your answers after you complete the exam. Take this time to correct any possible mistakes. Also, make sure that you have correctly transferred your answers for the multiple-choice questions to the answer sheet. And make sure you didn't skip a page. I encourage you to consider reviewing a few times if you have time left. I strongly encourage you to use all the time you have available to complete your exam and to review it.

48. Guide Your Team to Complete All Teamwork

Guiding your team's work does not mean leading your team. In fact, most of you don't like being told what to do, or having to report to someone constantly about what you're doing, or having someone always coming behind you checking your work or doing your work for you. That's why it's usually better if each person is responsible for his own work and there is no "team leader."

However, as my younger brother, Joel, said,

> *It can be beneficial to let the other team members know that you are available to help them, without imposing yourself on them. It doesn't mean that you lead your team, but you provide guidance if anyone wants it. You support the team and offer your help to the others if they need it.*

This way, you ensure that your teammates have the tools to do the job. Guiding your team's work is often the best method to use.

Why do you need to guide your team's work?

- To help move the work forward, if necessary.
- To avoid imposing yourself on others.
- To maintain a good relationship with your teammates.

How do you guide your team's work?

First, choose good teammates if you have the opportunity. If possible, choose the same type of team members as those individuals described in principle 43: "Consider Using a Study Group." In addition, consider students who have a variety of strengths, such as writing, computer skills, oral communication, etc.

Then agree together on a work plan. Here is a possible plan:

1. A first step may be to segment the work into smaller tasks. For example, these tasks can be to collect information, organize your ideas, make a writing or presentation plan, edit the work and revise the work.

2. A second step may be to divide these tasks between the team members as fairly as possible. Assigning the tasks based on each person's strengths or preferences is often a great way to do it. But if some team members' strengths or preferences are the same, randomly distributing the work may be preferable. Also, dividing a painful task among all team members is something you may want to consider.

3. A third step may be to determine an approximate time to complete each task. Then a fourth step may be to determine deadlines for each task. And a fifth step may be to plan group meetings to do follow-ups and put all your work together. A sixth step may be to provide an editing and revision period when the work is completed.

4. A final step may be to plan on completing and printing the work a few days in advance of the deadline. This will prevent something unexpected happening at the last minute and delaying your project. This could be something as simple as the lack of printer paper, lack of printer ink, etc.

Then write down your work plan, commit to each other to follow it from beginning to end and make sure all teammates have a copy.

Communicate often to avoid misunderstandings. Communicate your ideas and also your concerns, if necessary. But be sure to take time to listen, understand and consider the ideas and concerns of the others. And, of course, maintain a respectful attitude and tone of voice when you disagree with someone.

Finally, from the beginning of your project and all along the way, remind others that you are available to help in case they have difficulties, problems or concerns. Offer help, but do not impose yourself on anyone.

49. Finish Your Written Work a Few Days in Advance

Why do you need to finish your work early?

- To reduce your stress.
- To complete the work on schedule even if something unexpected happens.
- To be more confident.
- To finish and free your time to get started on your next tasks.

How do you finish your work early?

First, establish your work plan.

1. A first step may be to segment your work into smaller tasks.

2. A second step may be to determine an approximate time it will take to complete each task.

3. A third step may be to determine deadlines for each task.

4. A fourth step may be to plan to complete and print the final work a few days in advance.

Then, start on the first task the very first day your work is assigned. Remember principle 29: "Start Assignments Immediately."

Gather the information you need in order to create your work by using appropriate references, based on the level of credibility required. The most credible sources are those where it is most difficult to publish, such as scientific articles and reference books.

When collecting information, know how to quickly extract the desired information from a book. For example, in a book, search for a topic in the table of contents or search for key words in the glossary. Go to the relevant pages. Read introductions, conclusions and chapter summaries, or relevant sections. For more information, read the first and last sentences of paragraphs. For even more information, skim trough the whole text quickly.

Then continue and complete the work as quickly as possible. Work on getting things done for your project when you have long periods of time available. By working when you have longer periods of time, you will work more easily and quickly. You will already be in the mindset of your work and you won't have to constantly remember the context of where you were in the process.

Completing written work in advance is something that Cynthia does well. Here's what she told me:

> *In my anthropology class, I was assigned a project in September where I was required to interview someone from another country. This person had to share her immigration experience with me. She had to tell me what her immigration process had been like, if there had been problems, if she had to leave her family, or if she had a good experience and whether or not she had any regrets.*
>
> *I did not personally know any immigrants. But I did some research very quickly and discovered that one of my sister's teachers is an immigrant. So I interviewed her two weeks after the project was assigned. And I completed the project in September, even though the delivery date wasn't until December.*
>
> *My completed project was in my desk drawer until December and I was able to focus on my other assignments.*

50. Practice Your Oral Presentation

Why do you need to practice your presentation?

- To make a better presentation.
- To reduce your stress.
- To increase your confidence.

How do you practice for a presentation?

This approach is similar to the one for written work, except that instead of preparing a written project, you have to prepare a visual aid and practice your oral presentation. The visual aid is often a PowerPoint presentation.

Consider completing your visual aid and starting to practice your presentation as soon as possible. By doing this, you'll feel more in control, you'll be more confident, you'll reduce your stress and you'll have more time for your other assignments. When you have completed your visual aid, memorize the outline of the presentation to be sure you have mastery of your subject.

And consider these tips while practicing:

- take short breaths between each part of your presentation
- time yourself to fit within the allotted time
- if possible do your practices in the presentation room
- reduce your "uh's" and "um's"
- speak loudly
- speak more slowly than usual
- articulate your words
- vary the tone of your voice in order to emphasize what is important and to avoid putting your audience to sleep

Also consider these other tips while practicing:

- move away from the visual aid to avoid hiding it
- look at your audience
- practice in front of others and get their critique if possible
- incorporate humor when appropriate
- start your practice several days in advance

Also, if you have a visual aid, you should not need notes. But if you have any notes, do not read them.

These tips will help you prepare your visual aid:

- Make it clear, concise and visible to the back of the class.
- Make sure it includes the outline of the presentation and the references for your work.
- Also make sure that it works well the night before and the morning of the presentation.
- And as a precaution, have a copy of your presentation with you on a USB device and also email it to yourself.

You never know what might happen and those backups may come in handy.

And on the day of the presentation: be the first team to present if possible (it reduces anxiety and the stress of waiting), look at different people or at different places in the audience, and help your teammates in case they forget something while presenting.

I've seen oral presentations where one of the team members was presenting, then suddenly had a loss of memory and no other team member stepped in to help him. Yikes! It's embarrassing for the person who forgot, but also for the whole team that's not able to help him. Mastering your subject and understanding every part of your team's presentation will help you avoid this kind of embarrassment.

Finally, consider these tips for oral presentations presented by a team:

- divide the presentation equally between the team members
- make sure you understand each part of the presentation
- make sure to standardize all parts of your visual aid
- make sure as each team member completes his part, he briefly introduces the next teammate and what they will be sharing.

51. Prepare for Your Practical Exam

Practical exams are those that evaluate, among other things, your work method, your technical skills, and/or your ability to manage an unexpected situation or case. It may include laboratory work, clinical work, simulations, etc. This type of test is not found in all courses.

Why do you need to prepare for your practical exam?

- To make a better grade on it.
- To reduce your stress.
- To increase your confidence.

How do you prepare for a practical exam?

First, determine what the goals of your practical work are and make sure you can meet them. If necessary, consult the class syllabus. Then what you do will vary depending on whether or not you already know what you will be asked during your practical exam.

If you know the work that you will be asked to perform, you can better prepare. You can immediately establish a work plan, such as determining the steps to achieve the objectives, determine the time needed to complete the work, and determine the time required to complete these steps in the time you have available to prepare for the exam.

I encourage you to visualize yourself accomplishing your goals. You could also visualize yourself several times in the process of performing the required steps. I also encourage you to practice as often as possible. The more you practice, the more comfortable, and confident you'll feel and the more likely you are to succeed.

This is something that many dental students like myself have come to understand. Here's what Marie said to me:

For one of our dentistry practical exams, we had to cut plastic teeth.

I started practicing immediately and was cutting 10 teeth in half the time required long before my exam. I practiced cutting up several teeth many times until it was really easy for me. This allowed me to be 100% sure that when I took the exam, it would take me half the time and I wouldn't have to stress about it

And I also had the speed to be able to catch up in case I made a mistake. I made sure I had enough time to do it again. So I did a lot of practicing.

After Exams

The habits I suggest here will help you recover from your exams and prepare for your next semester.

52. Relax Right After Your Exam

Why do you need to relax after an exam?

- To maintain your energy.
- To remain productive after your exam.
- For your health and life balance.

How do you relax after an exam?

One thing you can do is to avoid comparing your answers with other students until you get your grade. Just like no two students studied exactly the same things for the exam, no students answered the exam questions exactly the same. If you compare answers, you could assume you gave the wrong answer and start being anxious until you get your grade. And if you fixate on it, you could lose your focus for your next presentation or exam.

Of course, this is also on a case-by-case basis. Some students will be reassured when they hear that other students answered with a similar response to theirs or when others also think that a question was rather odd. But some students easily worry and panic because their answers were different. Edith shares her experience on this subject:

> *I've done both: compared my answers with others and also avoided doing it.*
>
> *At first I was a student who asked a lot of questions after each exam and listened to the answers given by other students. I would get very stressed. And some students would grab their textbook immediately after an exam, trying to find answers to specific questions they didn't know.*
>
> *I decided those weren't the best approaches. So I started NOT comparing my answers after exams. Obviously*

when I had another class with the some of the same students right after an exam, I couldn't go very far, but there was always a way to avoid the comparison conversation.

And I tried not to look in my textbooks to find answers to specific questions I didn't know. I decided I didn't necessarily want to know the answers right away. It didn't do me any good and it only stressed me out to know I missed the answer. So I didn't do that, unless it was an extremely important question that I would need to know going forward.

I suggest that you leave your exam room immediately after the exam is over and that you resist the temptation to discuss your answers. Instead, take a moment to relax and take a break. Go reenergize, have a little fun and reward yourself for your effort.

53. Learn from Your Exam

Why do you need to learn from your exam?

- To improve how you do on future exams.

How do you learn from your exam?

First, find out the answers to important exam questions that you did not know. The important questions are usually worth a lot of points and they're usually information you'll need to know for your career. If you remember the question, find the answer in your notes, or other reference books. If you don't remember it, after you get your grade, check your exam and get clarification from the professor, if necessary. Then be sure you understand and memorize the answer. It's possible the same question may be found on your cumulative final exam.

Then, notice the type of questions that were on your exam and the length of the exam. There's a good chance these same types of questions will be found on your future exams with this same professor. And sometimes, you'll see that the questions are the same as on exams from previous years. This is what Alex realized:

> *When I realized that the professor asks exactly the same exam questions from previous years, I started getting the questions from previous exams and added them to my study material.*
>
> *In mechanical engineering classes, I was sometimes allowed to take into the exam one piece of paper with formulas and anything else I wanted to include on it. In these cases, instead of figuring out myself what to write on it, I wrote some questions/answers from past exams, such as confusing true or false questions. And this helped.*

54. Don't Worry about Your Classmates' Grades

Why shouldn't you find out what your classmates made?

- To keep you from comparing yourself to others.
- To reduce competition among classmates.
- To maintain your confidence when you get a lower grade.
- To avoid making other students jealous when you get a higher grade.

How do you keep from learning your classmates' grades?

If grades are posted in public or exams are handed back in class, try to look only at your grade. Of course, you may want to see what the average grade was, but avoid looking at individual students' grades. Try to keep your grades to yourself and avoid sharing them with other students. And don't ask other students what grade they received. But if someone really wants to share his grades with you, be polite, open and empathetic.

In my case, when I was in natural sciences, I initially compared my grades with other students. A lot of us did and it seemed natural, until I realized that it simply encouraged more competition among the classmates. In addition, it created or encouraged emotions that weren't always positive for me or for others, depending on whether my grades were above or below theirs.

When I realized that comparing grades didn't encourage anything good, I decided to keep my grades to myself in dental school.

55. Avoid any Drama about Your Grades

Why do you need to avoid drama?

- Because even if you get a lower grade, it's still a good score when you have higher grades for other exams or classes.
- To reduce your stress.
- To reduce competition and pressure.
- Because grades are not all that matters.

Although your overall GPA may help you get an interview, grades are not what will ultimately get you a job. Your attitude, your skills, your extracurricular involvement and your work experiences are also important.

How do you avoid drama?

Remind yourself that drama about your grades doesn't help. In fact, giving grades too much importance can be detrimental to you and your career. You could end up neglecting other important aspects of your life, such as your social life and your student involvement, and become unbalanced.

Recognize that you are imperfect and that you are entitled to some weaknesses. Nobody can perform perfectly 24/7. Getting a few lower grades is quite normal and shows that you are human. You are entitled to occasionally have less glorious moments.

Of course, this principle is for those who tend to place too much importance on their grades. This is not the case for all students, such as Marie, who told me:

> *I didn't have to have great grades. I tried to just compare myself to the average grade. And even then, I never*

gave my grades too much importance. If I had a lower grade on a test, I just told myself that I would catch up on the next test. I concentrated on doing my personal best.

56. Check with Your Professor if You Think Your Grade is Wrong

Why do you need to check on a suspect grade?

- Because errors happen.
- To correct an error and get your correct grade.

How do you check on a grade?

When you realize that there is a significant and unfavorable gap between the grade you thought you should have gotten and the one you received, go talk with your professor about your exam. Professors and university staff are human and can make mistakes. And if there is a mistake, ask for the correction and be sure to follow-up.

I had a big surprise one day when I saw a "D" on my online transcript for the exam that I was the most prepared for. In fact, my first reaction was to begin to doubt myself. Then I went to see my exam and realized that I got an "A+." What a relief! I later learned that all of that class's grades had been mixed up. But I had nothing to lose by checking.

57. Reward Your Efforts

Why do you need to reward yourself?

- To reward the child in you.
- To remain balanced.
- To stay motivated.

How do you reward yourself?

To celebrate any small or big achievement, give yourself a reward that will make you happy and that is proportional to your progress. This may be eating out, going to the movies, shopping for a few hours, having your family or friends over for dinner, or simply cooking your favorite meal for yourself. It depends on your personal preferences. Here's how Edith rewarded herself after her big exams in dentistry:

> *After exam week, I would always go buy a celebrity gossip magazine--those completely ridiculous magazines. I know what is written in them isn't true. But it was relaxing and fun for me to just read something completely stupid, which had no relation to my exams, and where I didn't have to retain any knowledge!*
>
> *I would read it at night on my sofa. It was non-intellectual reading. I found it so ridiculous to know that Britney Spears was seen eating a hamburger in a particular restaurant.*
>
> *In addition to those magazines, I would also spend time with my friends and my boyfriend–people I had been somewhat neglecting while I prepared for the exams. I would also go to the movies or out for dinner with friends.*

58. Organize Your Documents at the End of the Semester

Why do you need to organize your documents?

- To be able to find any document easily in the future.
- To officially end your semester.
- To help you move your focus to something else.

How do you organize your documents?

First, go through and throw out any useless documents, such as drafts, copies of notes, unimportant mail from your faculty, etc. Then, organize and store your important documents. For example, you could classify your documents and store them in your room library, or in filing cabinets or boxes. Finally, be sure to keep handy what you plan to use regularly in the future. You could, for example, keep close at hand your notes for a class that is continuing into the next semester.

In my case, I cleaned out my documents at the end of each semester. This increased my productivity, it gave me more space and allowed me to quickly prepare for the next semester. It was kind of like getting in the holiday spirit of Christmas or in summer vacation mode!

During Extracurricular Activities

Your involvement in extracurricular activities is crucial. As we'll discuss later, your grades will help you get an interview. Your grades show your prospective employers that you have the necessary individual skills, such as organization, logic, hard work and critical thinking. However, it is mainly your interactive skills that will help you get the job of your dreams. These skills are teamwork, leadership, communication and creativity.

In order to land the job of your dreams, you must prove to your employer that you have these skills. Your grades show your individual abilities. But your prospective employer will also want to see evidence of your interactive skills. And the best way to provide this is through examples of accomplishments in your extracurricular activities and work experiences where you demonstrated those skills. Let's talk about extracurricular activities you can get involved in and what you will learn from them.

59. Get Involved in Some Activities Related to Your Major

Why do you need to get involved in activities related to your major?

- To get to know your professors, your classmates, and the school faculty.
- So that those people can get to know you better.
- To develop a good relationship with them.
- So your professors will be able to write good reference letters for you later.
- So that your professors are more willing to help you in your studies and with your career.
- To establish connections with experts in your profession.
- To develop your teamwork and communication skills.

How do you get involved in these activities?

Participate regularly in events organized and offered by your school. This may be a fundraiser activity, a social event, or an evening conference about internships. Take advantage of these opportunities to build a relationship with your professors and other school faculty. You'll learn more about them personally and as a result may find that going to class is even more interesting because of the connection you have established with some of them.

Jean, a biology student, shares about a fundraising party he organized for students in his major:

> *I organized a fundraising party to help raise money for the department's welcome party at the beginning of the school year. I was in charge of the evening's entertainment.*

I organized an arm wrestling competition. I walked around and found out who was interested and then I paired them up and announced the participants for each round. It was very simple, but people had fun and it made them want to stay longer to see who would be in the final round.

It was a good opportunity for students to get together. And I think it's very important for students to attend these events.

By organizing this fundraiser, I developed my organization, communication, leadership and event management skills. It also allowed me to get to know my classmates better and to make good connections.

For the students that attended, it allowed them to develop some friendships, meet new people they have something in common with, and get to know them outside of class.

You may also want to pay attention to needed improvements in your department. If you find, for example, that your program is difficult and that students would greatly benefit from individual help, you could talk to the faculty and create a mentoring program where juniors and seniors are assigned a freshman or sophomore to mentor.

60. Get Involved in at Least One Committee, Club or Organization

Why do you need to get involved in one?

- To develop new relationships.
- To establish new contacts.
- To think about something other than school.
- To diversify your activities and knowledge.
- To develop your teamwork skills, communication and creativity.

How do you get involved?

First, at the very beginning of the school year, look for a committee, club or organization that interests you. It could be a first aid committee, a book club, an international organization, etc. Then attend a couple of meetings to find out what the objectives, expectations, needs, challenges and concerns of the group are. Then, join the group if it suits your needs and your interests.

Alex joined the aerospace group at his university. He explained:

> *They built a multi-stage rocket that worked with liquid fuel. The group was multidisciplinary. There were students in other majors of study that were involved. Initially, there were steps in the construction of the rocket that I didn't understand, because these steps were related to electronics. But I learned as I worked with the students in different majors.*
>
> *By doing this kind of project, I came to understand that some projects are very complex and it helped me develop*

project management skills. It also provided me with knowledge in areas that were not my main area of study.

Next, consider determining how you could improve your group, suggesting concrete actions to improve it and helping the group to achieve these actions. For example, if you belong to a book club where the books only interest a few of the participants, you could offer to do a survey with club members and make a list of their book preferences.

61. Consider Participating on a Sports Team

Why should you participate in sports?

- To stay fit.
- To develop new relationships and new contacts.
- To motivate yourself to exercise.
- To develop your teamwork and communication skills.

How do you get involved in sports?

Apply the same process as you did on the previous principle. Your sports team could be an intramural basketball team, a crossfit group or just a walking club. It could also be a cheerleading team, like Edith joined. Here's what she shares:

> *I made the cheerleading squad while I was studying physiotherapy. It was fun to spend time with the group. It made me concentrate on something other than my studies.*
>
> *I was also spending time with people who weren't in the same field of study as I was so I wasn't always hearing and talking about my major. Often the discussions were about sports. It gave me an opportunity to talk about something else that was more enjoyable.*
>
> *And even though people had different majors, they were still able to help each other. Whether you're studying engineering or human relationships, someone's going to have a relationship issue or an engineering problem at some point in time. In my case, people would ask me questions related to dentistry. I shared my knowledge and I was like an expert because I was the only member who was in the school of dentistry. It was really nice.*

Also, the team spirit was fun. Everyone supported everyone else. I felt like everyone was proud of me whenever I made an accomplishment for the team.

62. Consider Taking a Leadership Role in at Least One Group

Why do you need to take a leadership role in a group?

- To get more involved and be able to make more improvements in the group.
- To develop your confidence.
- To develop your leadership, teamwork and communication skills.

How do you take a leadership role?

Apply a principle similar to the previous principle.

Consider the groups (committee, club, organization, team) that you joined. Make sure you understand the objectives of these groups and learn about the various positions of responsibility in each group, such as president, vice president, secretary or treasurer. Next, determine the position and the group whose responsibilities best match your interests and would help you develop the skills you need most. At the next opportunity, let the appropriate people know you would like to fill this position.

My brother Jean has been in the biology department's student association for the past two years and is now the Treasurer. He tells me:

> *I am the Treasurer. My major responsibility is to plan the budget. I am also responsible for keeping the records regarding our department grants. I keep good records of all the money that goes in and out. Then, based on that, I help decide if there is enough money to do a particular activity. We're a team and everyone helps everyone else.*

This opportunity teaches me to be very organized. Before this I wasn't very good with numbers. Now I am. I also find it very fulfilling to be able to organize activities where everyone has fun.

What I like the most is that it helps me get to know almost all of the students in my department. I talk with lots of people and get to know what their interests are. After that, we arrange to meet their needs or offer something of interest to them.

For example, if I feel that there is something I would like to do, I ask other people. If there are a lot of people interested in it, then we try to do it. We want to make sure that it's something the students in the program will enjoy. I also find that organizing activities creates a more cohesive student body in general.

Again, look for ways to improve your group by making concrete suggestions for change and then helping achieve those changes. For example, if you're the Secretary and you find that the minutes taken by past secretaries are messy, you could suggest creating a guide to be used by the current and future secretaries. And you could offer to create the guide.

63. Withdraw from an Extracurricular Activity if Necessary

Why do you need to withdraw from an activity?

- To quit an activity if it does not interest you.
- To quit an activity if it keeps you from achieving your priorities.

How do you withdraw from an activity?

Decide if you can accomplish your most important priorities while still being involved in your extracurricular activities. For example, are you able to successfully study for your exams even if you are part of the newspaper committee, the soccer team and the photography club? Also, determine if your activities are still motivating you and still interesting to you. Do you still enjoy being part of the hockey team, the dance class or the first aid committee?

If you find that an activity prevents you from accomplishing your priorities, quit it and focus on your most important priorities. Similarly, if an activity no longer interests you, feel free to stop participating in it. If necessary, find a new activity that interests you more and join that one.

Alex told me that he once quit a student activity that no longer interested him:

I was a member of the Society of Automotive Engineers (SAE), but some of the other members were really snobby people. They thought they were really cool and their feelings of superiority really pissed me off. Especially since there were only 2-3 members who really were cool and who were moving our project along. The others, who thought they were the best, were just tagging along and weren't even working on the project. I wasn't interested in spending any more time with so many snobby people, so I left the group.

During Work Experiences

As extracurricular activities, work experiences can demonstrate to prospective employers that you have all the skills they are seeking. Work experiences can be paid work, paid or unpaid study or research internships, and volunteering. Your volunteer work, work experiences or internships may take place during your summers or during the school term. Let's see how to make the most of your work experience opportunities.

64. Consider Participating in an Internship Abroad

Going to another country can be a very rewarding experience. You may learn a lot about yourself, such as discovering some strengths and new interests. You may also become more aware of your weaknesses and your flaws. Also, because you are out of your comfort zone, you could be pushed to develop or improve certain skills, attitudes or habits.

It's also a golden experience that probably won't happen again in your life. It's typically only during college that you have the opportunity to travel for a long period so inexpensively.

Why do an internship or study abroad?

- To apply your knowledge somewhere else.
- To discover a new culture.
- To discover the world and expand your horizons.
- To develop new relationships.
- To take the opportunity to travel.
- To develop your confidence and skills, such as communication and organization.
- Because it's an opportunity that will probably not come again in your life.
- To enrich your life experience.

How do you do an internship or study abroad?

Start looking for opportunities to intern or study abroad as soon as you start your first year. Learn all you can about the host country, the host universities, objectives, expectations and pre-requisites of the internship or study program. Then attend the activities and presentations related to those abroad programs, and also question students who have previously participated about their experience in the program. Then choose your preference for the location and program, fulfill the necessary prerequisites, apply before the deadline and enjoy this amazing experience!

It really is a rewarding experience. I could never have imagined what an incredible experience it would be to spend three months during the summer in Europe in a French university. It was the best summer of my life. I had never been out of Canada and had not yet left the nest. This internship experience took me out of my comfort zone and pushed me to develop my confidence and my problem-solving skills.

In my internship I worked about 5 half-days per week in a healthcare center and a hospital. I was exposed to different clinical working methods and met, among others, a very generous student who invited me to her hometown. In addition, I took advantage of my free 4-5 days per week to explore Europe by train. I went to Italy, Belgium and Switzerland with just my backpack. I met great people who were also traveling who shared their life stories with me as if we were long-time friends. It was great. I recommend this unique experience to everyone!

65. Consider Getting Involved in a Research Project Related to Your Major

This especially applies if your major is in the sciences.

Why do you need to participate in a research internship?

- Because research projects are where a lot of real education takes place.
- To develop new relationships with experts in your field.
- Because your experience on a research team is considered very valuable by your prospective employers and by many graduate programs in the sciences.
- To develop your critical thinking, teamwork skills and creativity.

How do you participate in a research internship?

Apply the same process as with the previous principle. Your research internship could be working in laboratory manipulating test-tubes, working outside in the field to collect specimens, or working in a clinic taking data directly from real patients. The possibilities are innumerable.

You could have all sorts of surprising experiences. Here's an adventure that happened to Jean during his research project in biology one summer:

> *I was working in the forest with other teammates, luring bears into cages. Then we would collect their DNA from the fur they left behind so we could track their travels.*
>
> *Each day we prepared our equipment and went to collect the bear fur. My job was to put the lure into the cage. Meanwhile, my colleagues collected the data from the fur we collected.*

Once I heard a noise and assumed it was my teammates. After hearing it three times, I looked back and saw a bear. A huge bear, with his teeth chattering loudly–a show of intimidation. It was one of the biggest bears, if not the biggest, we had seen all summer.

I calmly told my teammates, "You need to get up slowly, don't move too quickly, because there's a bear." They didn't believe me at first. But when everyone realized there really was a bear, we got up, we got together, we stayed calm and we each spoke aloud each detail of what we were doing to make sure nobody panicked.

Everyone was very attentive and we paid attention to the tone of each other's voices to be sure nobody was panicking. It was very stressful, but we remained in control. We were careful and we did what had to be done, each one saying aloud what they were doing as well as what the bear was doing.

We managed to get around the bear and return to the vehicle. Once we got in the car, we started laughing–mainly because we were still full of adrenaline.

It was a great adventure. We learned the importance of staying calm during emergencies. We analyzed the situation and reacted properly to the problem. And our good communication helped us tremendously.

66. Get Involved in a Rewarding Summer Job

Why do you need to get a summer job?

- To discover the work environment.
- Because you have fewer obligations and more time to work during the summer.
- Because you'll have more time to get involved and help improve your workplace.
- Because you want to choose a job that will develop your skills and contribute to your fulfillment.

How do you get a summer job?

Start in January researching the job opportunities for the coming summer. Consider applying for multiple jobs that will be available. Find out what the tasks and prerequisites are of the positions that interest you. Ask prospective employers for more information, if needed. Consider asking former student employees about their past experience with certain employers, if possible. Then make sure you meet the prerequisites.

Be sure to apply for the positions that interest you before the deadline. After being hired, discover what the objectives, expectations, needs, problems or concerns of your team are. In the same way outlined in some previous principles, consider determining in which ways you could improve your team, suggesting concrete actions to improve your team and helping to achieve these actions.

In my case, my major focuses on ensuring that students become excellent clinicians after graduation. Although we are trained to have very good technical and clinical skills, we do not receive any training on the art of managing a clinic. Yet our work environment also includes a very important administrative side. So I took the opportunity during the summer to work as an office agent for the government in order to develop some administrative skills.

67. Reduce Your Work Hours when Studying Full-Time

Why do you need to reduce your work hours?

- To prioritize your studies and extracurricular activities, and/or your internships.
- To stay balanced.

How do you reduce your work hours?

If you work to pay for your college expenses, consider other possible ways to finance your education. There are, among other ways, loans and grants from the government, scholarships offered by your university or other organizations, voluntary financing from your family or parents (or even a loan from your family members), and loans or lines of credit. You have much more to gain in the long term by these other ways of funding, which will allow you to optimize your studies.

Also, if your finances allow you to reduce your work hours, negotiate with your employer to reduce your hours. If it is not possible, I suggest you consider leaving your job or finding another one with fewer hours. Definitely reduce your hours to minimum during exams. And even consider the ideal situation: to avoid working while you're taking classes. The long-term benefit is huge.

Edith shared one of her work experiences in the army reserves:

> *We were doing simulation exercises on weekends. Those are weekends when the army wants all their personnel to be present because those are extensive exercises to accomplish. We go into the woods with large vehicles and*

tents. Often these include enemy simulations among other things. We live in the woods and don't get a lot of sleep. We had to get up during the night. It was very stressful and demanding.

Those were well-paid and exciting weekends. They were a lot of fun because we had unique experiences, and we did it with a team. Everyone supports and looks after each other. But after those weekends, I was always exhausted and not able to function properly for the rest of the week. It took more than one day to get over it. It was hard on my week and on my studies. Over the weekend, I couldn't read or study anything, because I did not have a minute to myself. There was always something to do. And I was always moving. I found it too difficult. So I had to say no to some of those weekends.

I had to explain to my supervisors that I couldn't go because it was hurting my studies. But I also wanted to stay in the army. So I told them: "This particular month the exercise is at the same time as my exams, so I can't go. And I can't go on the next one because I have a lot of work that's due. But I can participate on these other weekends." I came up with solutions to accommodate them and me. By doing this, they were more open to discussion and understood what I was experiencing.

That experience helped me learn to talk to supervisors. Sometimes they are intimidating, especially in the military, because there are ranks. But that does not mean I'm wrong or I'm not smart. I just had to properly assess the situation and prepare what I needed to say and, after that, I could talk with them the right way.

68. Volunteer with an Organization You Believe In

Why do you need to volunteer with an organization?

- To help others.
- To give back to people some of what you have been fortunate to receive.
- To develop your selflessness and your creativity.
- To develop your self-worth and your confidence.

How do you volunteer?

Apply the same process as in principle 66: "Get Involved in a Rewarding Summer Job."

For example, Edith was volunteering in a field related to sports:

> *When I was in physiotherapy, I was volunteering for youth sport team competitions. I was part of the medical staff for football and soccer teams in elementary schools and in high schools. I supervised teams during the championships and I made bandages to treat wounds or to help prevent them. I was also trained to give first aid if there was, for example, a person who had a concussion. I loved doing it because it was connected to sports.*
>
> *This volunteering was important for me also because it was something that I could put on my resume and it was also super helpful for my career. On my resume, it showed that I had already provided these services with sport teams and that I had shown interest in things besides my studies. For my career, it was completing my knowledge in*

prevention and in trauma, because I was putting all my knowledge into practice.

It was also very rewarding as an experience. For example, I had a case of a dislocated shoulder. The person was in a lot of pain when I arrived. I was able to reposition their shoulder and they felt tremendous relief. They thanked me very much and I thought, "Wow, I really helped this person." It was a very good feeling.

This principle ends this section on habits to adopt to succeed in your studies. Habits are the regular actions that bring you closer to your success. But to achieve success, we have to combine these actions with the skills sought by employers in addition to a winning attitude.

PART FOUR: DEVELOP THE NECESSARY SKILLS

"It is possible to fly without motors, but not without knowledge and skill."

Wilbur Wright

The second variable in the college success formula is the development of the skills necessary to succeed, not just in school, but in all areas of life. These skills include organization, communication, hard work, logic, teamwork, critical thinking, leadership and creativity.

These skills are important because they will help you succeed in your career, whether you are an employee or employer. On the one hand, these are the skills that employers are looking for in their employees. And, on the other hand, these are the skills that employees are looking for in their employers. These employers may be business entrepreneurs or they may be graduate programs that you are involved with prior to beginning your career.

Employers know that these are the skills that contribute to the success of their companies or institutions. And employees know that these are the skills that contribute to their fulfillment and happiness at work. Since most of you will probably be working for an employer eventually, I will focus on these skills, because of their tremendous contribution to the success of your employer's business.

The skills sought by employers can be divided into two groups: individual and interactive. Individual skills allow you to be organized, to think logically, to work hard and to have good judgment. As for interactive skills, they allow you to work well in a team environment, to competently lead a group, to speak properly and to be able to creatively solve problems. Many of these skills and its importance, among others, have been highlighted in the book *Making College Count: A Real World Look at How to Succeed In and After College,* written by Patrick O'Brien.[3]

Individual skills are organization, logic, hard work and critical thinking. It is mainly the academic environment that supports your development of these skills. The interactive skills are teamwork, leadership, communication and creativity. It is mainly your extracurricular activities and work experiences that support your development of these skills.

And it is all of these skills, individual and interactive, that employers are looking for in job interviews. Generally, good transcripts demonstrate that you possess individual skills. But your achievements in extracurricular and work activities demonstrate that you have the desired interactive abilities. Usually your grades help you get an interview, but your achievements outside of academia help you get the job.

Therefore it is vitally important that you get involved in all three college arenas: your education, extracurricular activities, and the work environment. This is how you will develop all of the skills necessary to get good grades, provide tangible evidence to your prospective employer that you have the desired interactive skills, increase your chances of getting the job, and help you attain a great career. In fact, these skills are key elements to building a promising and prosperous career.

Part Four Contents

69. Organize Your Time and Your Workspace

Why do you need to organize your time and workspace?

- To achieve all your important tasks on time.
- To work in an orderly environment.
- To reduce your stress, forgetfulness and frustration.
- To avoid procrastination.
- To quickly find everything you need.
- Because organized students do better than others in academics.
- Because your employers are looking for employees capable of performing their tasks on time.

How do you organize yourself?

A. Manage your time:

1. Day Planner

Get a day planner (physical or virtual) where you can see your week at a glance and where the hours of the day are shown for each day. Then, write down the following: the time when you wake up and start your day, the time when you stop working and the time you go to bed.

Also write down in your daily planner, time periods during the day when you have obligations, such as your classes, exams, activities, work and include the specific details of these obligations. For example, for your exams you could specify the study material, the percentage of the final grade, the duration, the day and time, and the location. For your classes, you could write down the length, the location and the reading assignments.

Mark in your daily calendar time periods to study for your classes, and periods of time for entertainment. When you schedule those time periods to work, make sure you assign to your tasks an amount of time that is appropriate as it relates to their importance. You might expect about two hours of work or study for a one-hour class, but it varies depending on the course and the student.

Next write down in your day planner the time periods when you are at work (job or internship), times to exercise, your days and weeks off, any important dates (birthdays, deadlines, annual holidays etc.) and appointments (dentist, doctor, friends, interviews, meetings, etc.).

Cynthia, a psychology student, talked about the importance of having a single planning tool:

> *I need to keep a record of all of my appointments and commitments in the same place that I keep my assignment deadlines and exam dates. This way I can be sure that nothing is scheduled at the same time.*

2. Wall Calendar

I also suggest you keep on your wall a reminder of all your important obligations. First, put on your wall a copy of your weekly class schedule. Then put on your wall a giant school calendar and write down: days and weeks off, exam dates and the percentage of the final grade, deadlines, appointments and important activities.

3. Lists

Create lists (physical or virtual) that you will keep with you. These lists will be additional reminders. These can be lists for your goals, purchases, small tasks that you can do wherever you are, important people to stay connected with, current projects, future projects, etc. Then, update your lists gradually as an action is completed or a change happens.

4. Routine

Try to establish a routine for some important aspects of your life. First, try to wake up, go to bed and eat about at the same time on weekdays and weekends. Next, each evening prepare for the next day. Then take about an hour on Sunday evening to review the week that you just completed, make a note of your uncompleted tasks and schedule your time for the coming week.

5. Task Management

Determine what your tasks are, put them in order of importance and assign time in your schedule to complete them, starting with the most important or most difficult one. Also, use the time of day and the location where your focus is optimal to work on tasks that require a lot of focus.

6. Long-Term Projects

Consider the following tips to better manage your long-term projects: plan any long-term work before you jump into it, segment it into several simple actions, schedule an arbitrary deadline for achieving them and start completing the first action immediately. Also, schedule long periods of free time to do your work and use your short periods of free time to do your smaller tasks.

7. Productivity

When you had planned to do a job that requires a lot of focus, but your focus is just not there, do something else useful, such as any easier task. Always do something useful unless it's time you've scheduled for entertainment.

8. Waiting Time

Reduce your waiting times (line at the cafeteria, line after class to talk to professors, waiting at dentist office, waiting at the bus station, etc.) as much as possible by coordinating your activities, your schedule and your travel accordingly. Then, use your waiting periods to achieve simple, short tasks.

9. Interruptions

Consider these tips to better manage your time when something unexpected happens. First, try to stick to your schedule. But if necessary, reschedule immediately any delayed work. In fact, adjust your schedule immediately when something unexpected occurs. Finally, learn to say "no" when you're invited to take part in an activity or attend an event when you don't have the time or interest.

10. Just Do It!

Manage tasks as they come to mind. When something pops in your mind for you to do, determine whether any action is necessary. If it is necessary and you are available, just do it right then. If it's necessary but you're not available, book a time in your schedule to do it or add it to your list of short tasks. If no action is necessary, get rid of that thought and focus on things that need to be done.

11. Ask Yourself:

- What is the best use of my time right now?
- Is the time it takes to perform a certain action worth that piece of my life?
- When do I wait the longest or waste the most of my time?
- How can I reduce my waiting time or use it to my advantage by doing something useful?

B. Manage your physical workspace:

First, consider these tips:

- throw away what you do not use and is not valuable to you
- make your bed every morning
- empty your trash can regularly
- dust your work area every week
- schedule a few minutes every day to clean up
- keep handy the cleaning equipment you use most often

Immediately after you use anything, put it back in its place–every time. If you keep losing things, it's because they're not in their place. So find them a place.

And whenever you have something in your hand, determine right then if it needs to be thrown away (and throw it away), if it needs to be stored (and store it) or if it requires further action (do it immediately or schedule a time to do it).

And consider using at least two file cabinet drawers with folders to organize all your documents. You could use a drawer for your current classes and include your course syllabus, lecture notes, summaries of your notes, assignments, etc. in a file folder for each class. You could use the other drawer for previous classes and documents related to your extracurricular activities, work, tax records and academic records.

C. Manage your virtual workspace:

<u>1. School Folders</u>

First, create on your computer a folder for your studies. In this file add folders for your different years of study. For each year, you could add a folder for academics, a folder for the extracurricular activities and a folder for the work experiences or internship. Then add other folders as needed.

2. Pictures/Email Folders

Second, do the same for your pictures and emails. For your pictures, create appropriate folders in your computer and on your smartphone. And gradually organize your pictures in their respective folder. Also create similar folders in your email account to organize your emails.

3. Email Management

Third, reduce the time spent checking your emails. When you check your emails, determine if it needs to be deleted (and do it), if it needs to be filed (and file it) or if it requires further action (and mark it with an indicator or file it in a folder for further action). And when the further action is performed, repeat the process.

70. Work Hard

This is hard work, which requires perseverance.

Why do you need to work hard?

- Because students who work hard do better in academics.
- Because employers are looking for employees willing to put a lot of effort into their job in order for the team and company to be successful.

Notice that these sought-after employees are those who are even willing to work extra hours to get things done. They are not the ones who automatically pack up their things and head out the door at the end of their shift.

How do you work hard?

Put yourself into the work and persevere! But don't forget to take time to have fun afterwards!

In my case, the most difficult course I had in college was a course in pathology. The amount and scope of the material I had to learn and understand was tremendous. But because of consistent effort week after week, I finally managed to study all of the material and I performed like never before. There were a lot of times I felt discouraged, but I kept on going. And it really paid off. I even won an award in pathology!

71. Use Logic

Logic is the art of solving a problem in an analytical way (problem solving). It is also the art of finding a coherent link between different pieces of information.

Why develop your logic?

- Because logical students (who can create associations between different items and find coherent solutions to the problems presented) tend to excel in academics.
- Because employers are looking for employees who can solve problems by themselves.

How do you develop your logic?

Always be looking for opportunities to create consistent associations between different pieces of information. For example, you may find links between the different parts of your study material that will help you understand the essentials of the course.

You can also create mnemonics or acronyms so you can remember the material being studied. The well-known mnemonic device "*__M__y __V__ery __E__arnest __M__other __J__ust __S__howed __U__s __N__ine __P__lanets*" helps students remember the order of planets revolving around our sun: Mercury, Venus, Earth, Mars, Jupiter, Saturn, Uranus, Neptune and Pluto. I encourage you to create your own mnemonics and acronyms for your study material.

Also, when you do problem solving, divide your problem into smaller problems. This will make problem solving easier and can be applied in several fields, including mechanical engineering. Here is what Alex told me about this:

One of the things I did was to make sure I understood the questions on my exams and in my homework assignments. I made sure I answered the right question. To do so, I would often take the question and dissect it. I would dissect every aspect of the question and divide it into sub-questions that I responded to. That way, I was sure that I was preparing myself to answer the right question.

72. Use Critical Thinking

Critical thinking is a kind of filter for the information you receive continuously every day. Critical thinking allows you to make a judgment on the relevance and credibility of information.

As you know, you are bombarded every day by huge amounts of information, whether in the classroom or outside class. Think about the information you see on television, read on the internet, are told by your friends or family members, etc.

All of this extensive information transmitted to you is not necessarily relevant to your goals. Also, you can't read and study everything. In fact, you should choose the information you are going to invest your time in, especially during college. And critical thinking allows you to make this important selection.

That's why this skill is particularly important in principles 5 ("Control Your Education"), 32 ("Select Key Material for the Rereading of Your Notes"), and 34 ("Determine If Your Reading Assignments are Worth Your Time").

In addition, all this information is not necessarily credible. It is easy to believe almost anything. Fortunately, critical thinking protects your thoughts, your knowledge and your identity by selecting the information it considers true or valid.

Also, critical thinking contributes to your fulfillment, because it allows you to critique yourself. It allows you to evaluate your successes and your mistakes. It helps to question yourself about the path you're taking, whether you're getting closer to your goals or if you're moving away from them.

In short, critical thinking is the freedom you have to question information, to decide what it means to you, to act accordingly and to feel comfortable about your actions, your decisions, and your consequences. And this will help reduce your anxiety.

Why use critical thinking?

- To better control your education.
- To reduce your workload.
- To protect your knowledge and identity.
- To self-critique and improve yourself.
- To reduce your stress.

How do you use critical thinking?

Discerning Information by Relevance and Credibility

First, be discerning about the information transmitted to you. Determine the relevance of the information. Ask yourself: is this information relevant to my education, that is to say, to my classes, my exams or my career? Of course, it may be difficult to recognize what is relevant for your career when you have no experience yet in the workplace in your field.

Next, determine the credibility of the information. Is the information true or not? Or maybe a little of both? To find out, ask yourself what is the source of the information and what are their limitations.

To determine the source of the information, ask yourself the following questions. From where and from whom did the information come? How was the information passed to me? How has the information been received? Was there any distortion of information between the source and its recipients?

To determine the limits of the information, ask yourself the following questions. In what context or under what constraints does this information apply? Under what circumstances does it not apply?

Subsequently, consider only credible information that you judge relevant to your education, according to your goals and your core beliefs. And invest your time there. In fact, in college this is the kind of information you should study.

Then, skip any information that is not credible or that you judge irrelevant to your education. Do not invest your time in it. Don't study it. It would be a waste of time.

Critique Yourself Constructively

Second, critique yourself. Critique your ideas, your beliefs, your knowledge, your values, your business, your actions. Obviously, this needs to be a constructive exercise!

Determine if you are pursuing the right course of action, surrounding yourself with the right people, feeding yourself with positive thoughts, doing the right things and doing them the right way, are efficient and effective, and getting closer to your goals or moving further away from them, etc.

I want to mention that not only should you know the limits of information, but you also need to know your own limitations. During one particular semester, I took a lot of classes. One of my classes, morphological sciences, had three sub-divisions: anatomy, embryology and histology. The anatomy portion required me to know hundreds of pages of a reference book by heart. However, not only was this anatomy subdivision less than 25% of my grade for the class and irrelevant for my career, but with my schedule, I didn't even have the time to read all those pages, much less memorize them. So I decided to skip all that reading and memorization and focus on the classes that were worth the trouble–those that were relevant to my career. And I still passed the anatomy exam just by using my general knowledge and life experience.

73. Develop Your Communication Skills

Communication is the art of expression. It includes at least five components: listening, reading, speaking, writing and non-verbal. Communication is an essential skill in life.

No matter where you work, in one way your job will look like everyone else's: solving people's problems. It can be a plumbing problem where the pipes in your bathroom are defective. Or it can also be a dental problem where you have a broken tooth.

To solve these problems you have to be able to communicate. You must listen carefully to other people's problems, understand their concerns and problems, and articulate your solutions to them, whether orally or in writing. Making consistent hand gestures as you talk helps the listener understand. The same process applies if you have to communicate your own problem.

A Dental Example

Take, for example, the case where you are a dentist and a patient who has lost a filling comes to you. First, you pay attention to the notes about his medical status in his record and you ask him if it needs to be updated. Let's say this is a patient you saw last year and whose records indicate that he is allergic to penicillin.

You listen carefully to his chief complaint. Why did he come to you? Even if he has lost a filling, the reason why he came may vary. He may have come to you because food is getting stuck in the space where the filling was or possibly because the tooth is causing him a lot of pain and he wants medication to relieve the pain.

Next, you examine the patient and determine the real problem. After you examine the area of his concern, you realize that the problem is a broken filling. You observe that there is no infection and the nerve of the tooth is healthy. The piece of filling that fell out has created a hole in the tooth. That hole exposes the sensitive part of the tooth and also causes the food to accumulate.

Then you must explain to your patient the possible solutions to his problem in a way he can easily understand. You may tell him you could make a filling, an inlay, an onlay, or a crown. You must also give more explanations so he can choose the treatment option that best fits his needs: the treatment steps, cost, duration, disadvantages, risks, etc.

Then you need to make sure that your patient understands the options and ask him to choose one of them.

Then you provide the treatment that he decided on (and he could also decide on no treatment) and clearly document in his file what you observed, discussed and did: patient complaint, exam, problem (diagnosis), proposed solutions (proposed treatment) and their explanations, treatment provided, instructions after treatment, etc. Documenting clearly what you have done allows another professional who reads this file to understand the treatment provided.

Failing to listen to your patient's complaint (listen), carefully reading the note mentioning a penicillin allergy (reading), making a careful examination of the situation, communicating the different treatment options and their details (speaking) or recording carefully the details of the appointment in the patient record (writing), can lead to unfortunate misunderstandings, having to re-do the treatment, damage to your patient's tooth and/or, on rare occasions, even a legal issue. That is one example why good communication is essential.

Benefits of Effective Communication

This example was in the field of dentistry, but similar analogies can be made for other professions. Effective communication reduces misunderstandings, errors and frustrations. It reduces the time lost to having to redo your work, manage your unsatisfied clients, etc. It increases your productivity and the satisfaction of your clients. And communication is important not only at work but also in your personal life, with members of your family and friends.

And it's important that you develop your communication skills outside academics. In fact, the academic area usually encourages reading and writing skills more while extracurricular activities and work promote listening and speaking skills more. Because you will spend a lot of time sitting in class having to read and write but not necessarily to listen to real problems and express your ideas clearly, I strongly suggest you develop your listening and speaking skills during your activities outside class and when at work.

Why do you need to improve your communication skills?

- To reduce errors and misunderstandings.
- To reduce the amount of time you waste.
- To create and maintain harmonious relationships.
- Because employers are looking for employees who can express themselves properly and effectively.

How do you improve your communication skills?

Be sure to include an extracurricular activity or job in your schedule, allowing you to develop your listening and speaking skills. For example, you may join a choir or a local Toastmasters Club. Or you could work as a tour guide, an activities director for a summer camp or a receptionist. Activities and work that value listening and speaking are everywhere and can take different forms. I'm sure you can find one that interests you.

74. Develop Your Teamwork Skills

Good teamwork means being able to sacrifice some of your personal interests to a common and nobler interest. It is the art of compromise. It is also taking the place assigned to you in a group, whether you are the person who leads or the one who follows.

In the same way as communication, teamwork is needed in the workplace, and in life in general. In face, no matter what profession you're in, you will work at one time or another with people. This is the case whether you're a teacher, doctor, engineer, lawyer, cashier, etc. Teachers work with students, parents, other teachers and other staff at educational institutions. Doctors work with patients, nurses, other doctors and other staff at health institutions or clinics.

In your personal life, you are also surrounded by people, whether they're your siblings, your parents, your spouse, your children, your friends or even your pet! You must compromise with each of them. This way, directly or indirectly, you are part of a particular team, in your personal life and also at work.

And it is important to develop your team spirit outside academics. The academic environment encourages more individual work and learning. Of course, there may be some teamwork in academics. But it's mainly outside of this environment that your teamwork skills will be better developed.

Why do you need to develop your teamwork skills?

- To make your relationships more humane and fair at work, at home and within your family.
- Because employers are looking for employees who can sacrifice some of their individual interests for the sake of their business.

How do you develop your teamwork skills?

Be sure to include an extracurricular activity or a job that values teamwork. It can be to get involved in an internship on a research team, participate in an intramural sports team, be part of a student association or get involved in a volunteer group.

Jean, for example, was on an intramural volleyball team. Here is what he shared with me about his experience on the team:

> *My friends and I joined an intramural volleyball team at college. Since we know each other well, the communication on the field is really easy. And when we played, we had fun and laughed a lot. We encouraged our teammates, whether they made the shot or not. Even if someone missed his shot, we said, "Don't worry about it. You'll make it next time." We cheered for him and kept smiling. That was motivating.*
>
> *And every week we played another team. With our teamwork skills, we even won the tournament for the last two semesters. There were 8 teams and we ended up in first place twice. Our name is on the small trophy at the school.*
>
> *Being a part of team sports allows you to learn to look beyond yourself and to help others excel as well. It is a kind of cooperation on the team. Ultimately, it's often what makes you win, because you cannot win alone. You need the entire team and teamwork makes the difference.*

75. Develop Your Leadership Skills

Leadership is the art of influencing others: bringing them together, getting them to adopt your ideas, getting them to unite and work with you toward the realization of the objective you are promoting. It is when you become a leader that you are able to change the world, either by changing people's mindset or by accomplishing great things that would not have been done without the efforts of a team.

Just like the previous two principles, it is mainly outside academics that your leadership skills will be developed. Obviously it is possible to develop your leadership skills by being the president of your class or the leader of a study group. But extracurricular activities and working environments offer more of those opportunities.

Why do you need to develop your leadership skills?

- To learn how to unite people and influence them.
- To accomplish great things through the power of teamwork.
- Because employers are looking for individuals who can influence and motivate employees to achieve their business goals.
- Because it is an essential skill to have if you decide to go into business.

How do you develop leadership skills?

In the extracurricular activities or work environments that you participate in, look for a position that includes the power to make decisions and to influence the actions of a group of people. These positions bear significant responsibility in the group and allow you to make things happen.

In extracurricular activities, it can be filling the offices of president, vice-president, treasurer or secretary of a committee, organization or club. In the workplace, it can be a supervisor, manager, assistant manager or department head. It could also be to start your own business if you have the entrepreneurial spirit and you have noticed an unmet need around you. The possibilities are endless.

I know that even though this skill is important to develop, not everyone will see the value of developing it. Some of you may prefer to be followers instead of leaders. You may not see a need to develop your leadership abilities. And if being a follower makes you happy, that's good. But I still encourage you to try to develop your leadership skills, because you may discover that these skills will improve your life and contribute to your contentment and possibly even your success.

Jean, for example, is involved in a leadership role planning an interuniversity conference. Here is what he shares with us about his experience in that role:

> *I am currently in the process of organizing an interuniversity conference of biology students for the entire province of Quebec. This conference will be held during a weekend, from Friday to Sunday, and I am responsible for its organization.*
>
> *I am responsible for obtaining sponsorships. I am also supervising all of the organizing committees. One of my major tasks is to book hotel rooms to accommodate all students for the weekend. I am also organizing the activities and meetings for the weekend.*
>
> *On Friday, I will welcome the students from all the different universities. There will be a Friday night dinner, followed by several activities, which I am now planning.*

These activities, including dancing, will last until late at night.

On Saturday, several speakers will make presentations about biology. These speakers will be professors working on marine projects. Later in the afternoon, we will provide a variety of organized activities and sports events, such as an ice canoe race. Points will be awarded to the winning teams.

Then, on Saturday night there will be another dinner where the different universities will each give a presentation about their institution. Sunday morning will include breakfast, a closing ceremony and an awards ceremony.

76. Develop Your Creativity

Creativity is the art of inventing new things.

Like other interactive skills, creativity grows mainly outside the academic environment, with the exception, perhaps, of majoring in the arts or participating in a research project.

This skill is classified as interactive. Even though it's possible to create new things to help yourself, it's even better to create new things that help other people. When what you do helps others, then you really improve their individual lives, help improve the world around you, and contribute much more to your own fulfillment.

Why do you need to develop your creativity?

- To find new solutions to your existing problems and those of other people.
- Because employers are looking for employees who can bring new ideas, find solutions to problems and initiate them.

How do you develop your creativity?

Make sure you have at least one extracurricular activity or work environment that values creativity. This could be membership in an improvisation club, a social committee or a committee that organizes major campus events.

You might also look for unmet needs in your group. Then you could suggest improvements or solutions to those needs and help make those improvements. For example, say you're a member of the improvisation club and it has a serious lack of funds needed to finance its activities. You suggest organizing a comedy show as a fundraiser event, with reasonable prices for the students. You may offer to be in charge of organizing this event in order to develop your creativity even further.

Or you could create your own business, if you have the entrepreneurial spirit and if you have found a new solution to an actual problem. For example, you could start a computer services business for students.

And even though it's best to benefit others with your creativity, nothing prevents you from being creative just for you.

This is what Jean likes to do when he plays guitar at home:

> *Sometimes I sit down with my guitar and I'm not sure what I'll play, but I just start trying different things. Every once in a while I'm really impressed with what happens and I keep going in that direction. I'm always trying new things with my guitar. That's one way I'm develop my creativity–and it's just for me.*
>
> *Sometimes I try to replicate on my guitar different melodies and chord progressions that I've heard in music I listen to. Discovering new things allows me to develop my musical ability and creativity. And I'm becoming a better guitarist.*

Now you know what skills are valued in the academic arena and which ones are valued in extracurricular activities and working environments. By getting involved in these three areas, you will be able to develop all these skills, prove to your prospective employers that you have them, increase your chances of getting the job you want, and be successful in your career.

Part Five Contents

PART FIVE: ADOPT A WINNING ATTITUDE

"The greatest revolution of our generation is the discovery that human beings, by changing the inner attitudes of their minds, can change the outer aspects of their lives."

William James

Now you know that skills are an important variable in the college success formula. But that's not all! You must also develop a winning attitude before you can succeed. This attitude is necessary in order for you to succeed in your studies. But it is also necessary in order for you to succeed in your career, whether you are an employee or the employer. On one hand, it is this attitude that employers value in their employees. On the other hand, it is also this attitude that employees value in their employer.

The winning attitude can be developed in the three areas: academics, extracurricular activities and work. The successful student is curious, motivated, focused, disciplined, confident, honest, positive and ambitious. Let's start with the importance of being curious.

77. Stay Curious

Curiosity is the desire to learn something new. It is to be interested in learning.

Why do you need to be curious?

- Because curiosity helps accelerate your learning and learning helps improve your life.
- Because employers are looking for employees interested in their business and willing to keep learning and improving.

How do you stay curious?

It is easy to cultivate curiosity if you are naturally curious. But it's more difficult to do if you're not.

A good way to cultivate your curiosity is to understand the benefits it brings you. When you're interested in learning new things, you will discover new things. The more knowledge and experience you gain, the more tools you will have to solve your problems and the more you'll improve your life.

Also, the more you know, the more you'll realize that you don't know. You'll realize that knowledge and experience are vast and that there's a lot more you can learn that will improve your life even more. So the main benefit of curiosity is that it helps you improve your life.

Alex's curiosity was very beneficial in one of his classes:

I was very interested in my class on fluid mechanics. It was more complicated than my other classes. But because I was very interested in the subject, I found that it was easier to spend time studying the material. I really wanted to understand the subject matter, so I dug deeper and even studied 'ahead' of my class assignments. Soon I was memorizing the material, which really helped me in the long run.

78. Fuel Your Motivation

Motivation is what drives action.

Motivation and curiosity are tied very closely to each other. Motivation makes you take action and pushes you to learn and to keep on learning. Curiosity is one of the ways to stay motivated.

Why do you need to be motivated?

- To enjoy learning and learn more easily.
- Because employers are seeking individuals who are motivated and, even better, who are capable of motivating their employees to perform their duties.

How do you stay motivated?

1. Consider looking at the possible causes of your lack of motivation and find a solution.

   - Are you unmotivated because you're tired? You could relax and re-energize before continuing to work.
   - Are you unmotivated because you've worked too long without stopping? You could take a break, have fun and go outside for a breath of fresh air.
   - Are you unmotivated because you're working alone? You could join a study group.

2. Read and review your goals every day. Remember that why you do what you do is to achieve your goals. Also consider decorating your room in a way that stimulates you and reminds you of your goals. Regularly review the things that stimulate you, inspire you and remind you of your goals. If your goals no longer motivate

you, ask yourself if you have enough goals, if they are still relevant or if you should change them.

3. Make sure you keep yourself in a motivating and exciting environment. Make sure you are in a major field of study that interests you. Make sure you have friends and activities that motivate you. Consider getting involved in a big project that energizes you. Make sure that you surround yourself with positive, motivating and energizing people. And stay away from negative, unmotivated and depressing people.

4. Consider these next tips. Make sure that you have motivation before starting your work, in order to combine "work" with "motivation" and to avoid associating "work" with "boredom." Also, set deadlines for your tasks and reward yourself when you meet your deadlines or when you have made great effort. Also, set aside at least a few minutes each day for some entertainment.

Here's how Marie motivated herself to study:

> *I told myself that I would stop studying at 8pm and after that I would watch a TV show or go to the gym. I motivated and rewarded myself by exercising and watching my favorite TV shows.*

79. Boost Your Focus

Focus is the ability to fully direct your attention to a task.

Why do you need to be focused?

- To study and work more efficiently and faster.
- To reduce the amount of time you waste.
- To reduce the likelihood of errors in your work.
- Because employers are looking for efficient employees who can focus on their work and produce few errors.

How do you stay focused?

1. Avoid multitasking–trying to do several things at once. By doing several things at once, your focus is divided between several tasks and your productivity and attention is reduced.

2. Reduce the distractions around you when you work. You need to identify these distractions. It may be your phone ringing or vibrating, the opened inbox of emails, the audible alerts signifying new text messages or emails, your open Facebook account, the radio or television noise, the music from your electronic devices, etc.

Reduce or remove these distractions before starting work. You may need to turn off your phone, close your email inbox, turn off your radio or television, close your computer if you don't use it to study, or turn off your music devices. I need to mention that although music can be a source of disturbance for some people, it can also promote focus for others. This may be the case if you have a musical intelligence. Ultimately, it is up to you to know yourself and know what distracts you and act accordingly.

Marie is distracted by any disorder. She needs everything to be organized and orderly in order for her to study effectively:

> *When I was studying, all my binders needed to be arranged perfectly, in order from the first course to the last one. And documents had to be in date order in each binder. Also, my shelf on my bookshelf needed to be in perfect order and my workspace needed to be cleaned.*

Jean has a musical intelligence and listening to music often helps him focus.

> *I listen to music while studying or doing assignments. It helps me because it removes external noise and I feel completely isolated and focused.*
>
> *I listen to all styles of music while I study. I listen to rock music if I start feeling sleepy. I listen to classical music if I feel very inspired. I listen to blues if I feel a little too excited and it calms me down. I use different styles of music depending on my mood to optimize my study time.*

Also, when you are in the middle of working on a task and something suddenly pops into your mind that you have forgotten to do, write it down immediately. That way you will free your mind, increase your focus and don't have to worry about forgetting it again. And, when you have completed your work, you can then plan or perform any required action.

3. Reduce things that irritate you. Start by identifying these irritants: your messy workspace, defective items, missing materials, etc. Then reduce, remove or correct these irritants. This could be cleaning your workspace, repairing or replacing your defective items, purchasing your missing equipment or materials, etc.

4. Take a short break when your focus is poor and come back to work with more concentration. You want to associate "work" with "focus." You also want to associate "work" with "efficiency."

80. Practice Discipline

Discipline is respecting your commitments and goals. Obviously, this means your commitment and goals must be reasonable. Discipline is the opposite of procrastination (putting off the implementation of the commitments that bring you to your goals). Finally, it also involves respecting the commitments you have made to other people.

Why do you need to be disciplined?

- To complete your tasks, your studies and your work on time.
- To become a person who respects her commitments, a person others can trust.

How do you practice discipline?

1. Have a time on your schedule every day to work. Even if it is only for a few minutes. This way, you make sure you stay in the habit of working. Also make sure to always do something useful during your scheduled work time. And perform the most difficult tasks first, the ones you want to do the least and worry you the most. Get them done first, free your mind, reduce your guilt and move on to more interesting tasks!

2. Recognize that you need to take time to relax and entertain yourself in order to find the motivation and discipline to work. So also be sure to schedule time every day to relax and have fun. And remember that you need to be rewarded to stay encouraged to continue your efforts. So promise yourself a reward after you reach a deadline or goal.

Promising yourself a reward after a lot of studying is very popular. Previously we saw that Marie motivated herself with her favorite TV shows and training sessions at the gym. Let's how Jean rewards himself with sports after studying:

> *During winter exam week, I told myself, "Ok, I'm going to study all I have to study and then I'm going to take a little time to play some ball or at least get some fresh air." I love sports. I enjoy all kind of sports: hockey and volleyball are two of my favorites. And playing sports helps me focus. It helps me discipline myself to study and it helps me stay focused while I'm studying.*

3. Stop complaining about your workload and start completing your tasks. If you don't start or continue it, it will only accumulate. Also, stop finding excuses to not do your work, unless there's serious illness, a family death or something else catastrophic. And follow your schedule as much as possible. When you fall behind, adjust it so you can stay on time.

4. Recognize that procrastinating until the last minute doesn't make you work better. No one works best under pressure. Remember there are consequences of procrastination and working under pressure at the last minute: negative stress, anxiety, confusion, loss of control, poor quality of work, common mistakes, disappointment, guilt, loss of self-confidence. And it compromises your dignity, your pride and your honor.

5. Continue to visualize your goals. Remember all the reasons why you should persevere and remember the extraordinary career that awaits you if you continue.

6. Use feelings such as your dignity and honor to motivate you to be disciplined, to persevere and to fulfill your obligations.

81. Be Confident

Confidence is like insurance on your value. This is insurance that protects the value of your actions, your skills, your attitude, your habits and your core values, in case of any infringement on those values.

It is an insurance that you may decide to give yourself. But it is also an assurance that you may decide to receive from others. Some people become naturally confident, finding their confidence in themselves without the encouragement of others. While others need the support and encouragement from other people to build their confidence.

Developing your confidence does not come easy for everyone. Because some people are naturally confident while others doubt themselves, developing self-confidence is not the same amount of work for everyone. Some will have to work harder than others to obtain it. And it is a skill that can take a long time to be developed.

Why do you need to be confident?

- To be assured that what you do has value.
- To feel satisfaction in what you're doing.
- To protect your worth against those who don't believe in you or who may try to reduce your value.
- To allow yourself to express who you really are and to be authentic.

How do you develop your confidence?

Consider these tips.

- Remember that you are smart: you have different types of intelligence.
- Make a list of your strengths and skills and read it often.
- Make a list of your successes and read it often.
- Showcase your successes with a prize, a medal, a trophy, a certificate, a thank you card, etc.
- Practice an activity in which you are better than others.
- Realize that if you have been accepted into your program of study, you have the potential to succeed.
- Practice doing on a regular basis what you feel uncomfortable doing.

Here's an example from me. In high school I hated oral presentations. I was scared and I had stomachaches for several days in advance just thinking about it. I didn't really trust myself to do a good job. The following summer I did an English immersion where I had to make three oral presentations in one month. I was very surprised that during my third oral presentation I had a lot of confidence and I even had fun doing it. I realized that practicing in areas you are less confident in helps increase your confidence a lot.

82. Be Honest

Honesty is authenticity or integrity. It is to act in accordance with who you are, your values and your goals. But it is also to recognize the place you have in community. In fact, it is to realize that although you are intelligent and important, other people are, too. Each person is important, has value and deserves respect as much as you do.

Why do you need to be honest?

- Because the more authentic you are, the closer you will get to your goals.
- So that others have more confidence in you.
- To live in harmony with your values, beliefs and goals, and be happy.

How do you stay honest?

Be Yourself

Avoid trying to be someone else. Make sure you are yourself and learn to say no when someone offers you something that takes you away from your goals. Of course, it is easier to express who you are when you are self-confident. When you're sure of your value, you're not afraid of displeasing other people and you can express yourself freely without discomfort.

Accept Your Imperfections

Be true and respectful, to yourself and to others. Acknowledge not just your strengths, your skills and your successes, but also your mistakes and imperfections. Realize that you are not perfect.

Respect Others

Regarding other people, respect them. They deserve respect just like you do. They are just as valuable as you are. They have an ego just like you do. And they want you to highlight their successes just like you may wish them to highlight your own. Apologize sincerely for any mistakes you make that affect them. Don't be afraid to admit your mistakes, because it makes people more receptive to you and open to discussions or solutions you may propose.

Value Others

Sincerely congratulate others for their success. Don't be afraid to do this. Under no circumstances does valuing other people devalue you. On the contrary, others will be more willing to congratulate you for your own success if you compliment theirs. And you'll create and maintain more harmonious relationships. And don't intimidate or degrade another person. Doing this actually devalues you. Because what you do to others reflects who you are.

Here Alex shares an experience that shows how important he believes it is to praise other people's successes.

> *I often studied with a team, and one of my teammates was a girl who wasn't very good in class. In fact, she had a lot of difficulty. On her exams, she generally expected to get a grade of about 55%, while others of us on our team expected to get a grade of about 85%. Whenever she got 70%, I sincerely congratulated her, even if getting a 70% would not have been a good grade for me.*
>
> *It was important for me to celebrate her success with her because she was one of my friends, and it helped build her personality and self-confidence. It helped her become a solid person. And remember, these are people who later on*

will be able to help you in some area. So it's important to put yourself in their shoes, recognize improvements they have made, and highlight their progress.

And obviously, being honest is not cheating on exams.

83. Think Positively*

Being positive is easily finding reasons to be optimistic.

Why do you need to be positive?

- To feed your mind with positive thoughts.
- To do more positive actions and to speak more positively (because your thoughts dictate your actions and words).
- To become an enthusiastic and happy person (because you are the reflection of your thoughts).
- To inspire you, motivate you, energize you and contribute to your happiness as well as the happiness of others.
- Because positive, optimistic and happy students perform better.

How can you be more positive?

Consider these tips.

- Laugh every day.
- Set aside at least a few minutes every day to be entertained.
- Turn your negative thoughts into positive ones.
- Try to find something positive in every event and person.
- Try to find solutions to your problems instead of complaining about them.
- Believe that you will achieve your goals.
- Continue to visualize your goals and your future.

Here is Alex's perspective on positivism:

I try to be positive all the time because I've learned that being negative doesn't help me–it only adds to my stress.

For example, suppose I have an exam and my mindset is, "Oh, no! I'm going to fail this exam!"

Well, there's a chance I won't do well even if I know 90% of the material. If I come to the exam with a negative attitude and the first question on the exam is part of the 10% of the material that I don't know, I'll get stressed out and think, "I can't even answer the first question!" And I could possibly spend a lot of time trying to answer that first question that I don't know instead of moving on and easily answering 90% of the questions on the exam.

I've realized that being positive in college helps take away unnecessary stress and makes it easier to remove any obstacles in the way of my success. And being positive has no negative aspects!

84. Be Ambitious

Ambition is the desire to tackle challenges. It is the willingness to make additional effort to achieve a difficult and honorable goal. Ambition goes beyond curiosity (desire to learn) and motivation (what pushes you to act), because it is about challenging yourself. You will have to have ambition before you will leave your comfort zone to develop the necessary skills and tools to achieve your lofty goals.

The rapid acquisition of these tools and skills will also contribute to your long-term wellbeing by reducing stress, increasing your confidence and making you happier.

Why do you need to be ambitious?

- To develop new skills faster.
- To quickly develop the tools to help you better cope with the difficulties of life.
- To greatly improve in all aspects of your life.
- To increase your wellbeing.

How do you become ambitious?

The main thing is to be brave and look for challenges. This may mean taking the difficult class that interests you, taking the position of president in an organization, proposing and implementing changes in your community, starting your own business, participating in the annual faculty show, etc. In short, look for opportunities that push you out of your comfort zone and allow you to develop new tools that will help you achieve your life goals.

In my case, one of my goals at college was extremely ambitious: I wanted to graduate in the top 5% of my class. My course of study had a very limited enrollment and was a very competitive program. I knew it wasn't going to be easy because all of the students in my major were very talented. But I really wanted to set the bar high in order to push myself to excel and stand out. I was very excited when I reached this goal!

We have completed the fifth part. You have discovered that curiosity, motivation, focus, discipline, confidence, honesty, positivity and ambition are part of a winning attitude while you're in college. This attitude can be developed in the three different areas of academics, extracurricular activities and work. And this attitude is also necessary if you're going to have a rewarding career.

Part Six Contents

PART SIX: KEEP IMPROVING YOURSELF

"He who stops being better stops being good."

Oliver Cromwell

By applying the college success formula correctly, you will be able to succeed in many ways and at many levels in academics, in extracurricular activities and in the workplace.

However, your efforts and perseverance should not stop when you get a few successes under your belt. You should keep on trying to improve. The more you improve, the happier you'll be and the more you'll help others be happy. The more success you achieve, the more you'll be able to improve, and the process continues.

The wheel of improvement will continue to turn, move forward and carry you toward more happiness, but only if you have the will to keep improving–which I hope you do!

85. Learn from Your Mistakes*

Why do you need to learn from your mistakes?

- To avoid repeating them.
- To learn from them and improve.
- To convert your mistakes into successes.

How do you learn from mistakes?

At the end of each semester, do a self-assessment of the semester you just completed and evaluate any mistakes. Determine what your mistakes were. It may be failing to keep in touch with your family members because you were too busy. Then determine the unfavorable circumstances contributing to your mistakes. For example, it could be that you lacked organization and that's why you failed to make time for your family. Then decide how to correct and avoid these circumstances and these errors the next semester. For example, you could schedule a time in your daily planner each week to call a family member.

Edith shares one of her mistakes and what she learned from it:

I went to bed too late at the beginning of the semester when I was studying for an exam. I tried to read all my notes the night before the exam, but it didn't help me. My brain wasn't working properly the next day. I didn't even remember what I had studied because I was too exhausted. I realized that I wasn't able to function properly when I was going to bed so late.

When I realized my mistake, I quickly adjusted. In fact, instead of trying to study forever at night, I went to bed early and got up early the next day. Then I would study until

I had no more time and had to leave to go take my exam. This way I had time to review, I had all my brainpower, and I wasn't as tired and did much better on my exams.

86. Be Inspired by Your Successes

Why do you need to be inspired by your successes?

- To encourage yourself to repeat them.
- To learn from them and to improve.
- To increase your self-confidence.

How do you gather inspiration from your successes?

After learning from your mistakes at the end of each semester, like you did in the previous principle, also spend time looking at your successes. Determine what your successes were, or where you made definite progress.

For example, you may have received high grades in your art history class. Then look for the favorable circumstances contributing to your successes. Maybe you started studying for the exam several weeks in advance. Then plan to replicate these circumstances and these successes in the coming semester. You could start studying for your other exams early, too.

And I invite you to make a list of your successes and regularly review it to inspire yourself!

Alex shares how one of his successes inspired him:

> *My first year in software engineering was easy. But I realized I was in the wrong major because I really didn't like it. So I quit college for a year to figure out what I wanted to do.*
>
> *I knew that I liked math and mechanics and that I liked learning things. Then I realized that I wanted to be a*

mechanical engineer. However, I wasn't convinced that I wanted to go back to college for several years.

But then I remembered how easy college was for me that first year and that success motivated me to go back. I was accepted in mechanical engineering and I was so inspired that I graduated a year before everyone else in my class. I completed a four-year program in three years!

87. Recognize the Value in the Differences of Others

Why do you need to value others' differences?

- Because others are there to challenge who you are and help you improve.
- Because the strengths and differences of others can supplement your strengths and improve your weaknesses.
- Because bigger successes are achieved when a group of people combine their strengths and differences to achieve a common goal.
- Because others can be a great source of support, help, motivation, confidence, friendship and love.
- Because others have a lot to teach you.

How do you value others' differences?

Consider these tips.

<u>Thank Your Critics</u>

Sincerely thank the people who suggest ways for you to improve, rather than being on the defensive. It may be a friend who tells you that you should take time to listen to others more. It may be your mother who tells you that you tend to neglect your family. Those critics can help you become a better person. Of course, you need to decide if their comments are true or not. But whether they are true or not, you should thank the person because they're showing an interest in you.

<u>Express Gratitude</u>

Remember to thank others for any services they render you. It may be a classmate who lends you his notes because you were absent. Or a friend that brings you coffee. We don't always appreciate others enough. Thanking people shows them that we appreciate what they do for us and how they enrich our lives. In fact, showing gratitude always paid off and there are no negative consequences.

Value Our Differences

You also need to value the differences in other people. It can be by making sure to use each other's strengths as much as possible when working on a team. If you have a teammate who is a great researcher or one who is an excellent writer, look for opportunities to take advantage of their talents. This way, you get a much more impressive result than if you had done it all alone.

Here's how Alex used this principle:

> *I was on a team with just two members. My teammate was really good at doing the layout of the reports. He was extraordinarily talented in that area. So he did the layout while I was doing the calculations. I was doing the content of the report and he was making like the container. It was great.*
>
> *I like to encourage my teammates' strengths when working on a project. The goal is not really to point out the differences, but rather to encourage them, because these differences that my teammates have are often weaknesses I have. And that way, my weaknesses are often compensated for by other team members!*

Ask for Help

Finally, don't be afraid to ask for help or advice from others. Others are there to help you grow. They have knowledge and skills that you don't have, that might be useful for you and that you could learn to develop further. If you get a computer virus and don't know how to get it out from your laptop, why don't you ask the computer guru in your class? He'll probably be glad to help you and you may learn something in the process!

88. Seize Great Opportunities

Why do you need to seize opportunities?

- Because the same opportunity only comes around one time.
- Because you shouldn't sit by and watch someone else take advantage of the opportunity instead of you.
- Because those who succeed are the people who immediately seize the great opportunities that come to them.

How do you seize an opportunity?

First, recognize that opportunities are all around you. There are way too many for you to accomplish. Then open your eyes and ears and examine any good opportunities that come your way. You might read in your school newsletter that the next career day will provide an opportunity to meet dozens of respected companies in your area. It might be the place you meet your future employer or business partner.

Then, when you see an opportunity, take the challenge and do it. Don't hesitate and wait for a better one to come along. Say you're studying to be a translator and want to work for a translation company in your area, but there is not one. Consider starting your own business in your area if there is a market for it.

Here's a great opportunity Edith seized during dentistry school:

> *During my summers, I worked as a dentist for the army reserves, even though I was still in school. Normally, in the dental program, there are certain dental treatments we can start doing beginning in our fourth year. But because of*

my position in the army, I had already done several of these procedures before my fourth year.

During the summer between my junior and senior years, I worked at a local dental clinic and the senior dentist had hurt her thumb. She planned to cancel her entire schedule, but rather than doing that, she asked me if I wanted to take over her schedule. She said that she would supervise me. I told her I didn't feel very comfortable doing all of the procedures. But she said: "You are capable. And I'll be right next to you." So I finally agreed to do it.

So I took care of her patients that summer. She supervised me, stayed in the room with me, and kept notes on the procedures I did. That summer, I cemented my first crowns and did a lot of new procedures. It was extremely interesting. It was like I had a personal coach!

89. Reduce Your Stress

Why do you need to reduce your stress?

- To be more in control of whatever you're working on.
- To reduce the likelihood of errors.
- To work more efficiently, quickly and easily.
- To protect your health.

How do you reduce your stress?

Everyone doesn't have the same ability to handle stress. And based on the goals individuals set for themselves and the depth of their self-confidence, stress levels will vary. However, all the habits, attitudes and skills we discussed previously will help reduce your stress.

Remember these good habits: visualizing your goals, exercising, getting enough sleep, eating well, drinking water, working when it's time, entertaining yourself when it's time and surrounding yourself with positive people. Also remember these skills: be organized, work hard, use critical thinking, be logical and communicate effectively. And finally, remember the elements of a winning attitude: be disciplined, be confident and be positive.

I want to take this opportunity to mention that for many students, physical exercise does the best job to reduce stress. This is the case with Jean:

> *Playing sports is my best stress reducer. It is the endorphins. I exercise in some way almost every day. After exercising, I feel relaxed. It removes all unnecessary stress and I am able to focus on what matters. The sports I play are volleyball, rock climbing, hockey, biking, among others. I*

play a wide variety of sports all the time. For example, during a semester, on Monday I may play volleyball, and on Wednesday I may play hockey. Other times during the week, I may do rock climbing or biking. They all help me keep my stress under control.

90. Aim for Excellence

Excellence is the passion to always do well. It is to constantly strive to improve yourself and your work.

Here is how Alex defines excellence:

Excellence is to work hard to compensate for and strengthen your weaknesses, and to try to improve yourself. For example, I made a mistake when I didn't ask the professor directly in class what a gyroscope was. But I learned. Excellence is now asking questions as soon as I don't understand something important.

Why do you need to aim for excellence?

- Because it is a possible, positive and worthy objective.
- Because it helps to improve you and your life.
- Because it will lead you to discover more success down the road.

How do you aim for excellence?

- Always be on the lookout for how you can be an even better person tomorrow than you were yesterday.
- When you make mistakes, learn from them and avoid repeating them.
- Continue to make progress and motivate yourself as you continue moving forward.
- Keep moving forward in spite of your mistakes and your successes.
- Surround yourself with people who are better than you.
- Have ambitious goals and projects that will push you to improve your attitude, skills and habits.
- Always stay curious to learn new things and meet new people.
- And keep fueling your motivation. Don't lose your motivation.

91. Avoid Perfectionism*

Perfectionism is striving for the impossible realization of absolute quality.

Why do you need to avoid perfectionism?

- Because it is an impossible objective.
- Because it contributes to discouragement and depression.
- Because you will focus more on disappointments and mistakes instead of progress and success.
- So you can continue to move forward and grow in spite of your imperfections and those of others.

How do you avoid perfectionism?

1. Shut up that little voice in your head that is always dissatisfied with your work, study, reading, achievements, yourself and even other people. Here's how Marie applies this principle.

> *When I studied, I studied to understand the material and to learn the important details I needed to know for exams. Once I understood the material, even if I only got an 80 instead of a 100, it didn't upset me. I would tell myself: "I got an 80. I'm average. That is good enough! I'll make a great dentist!*

2. Acknowledge and agree that perfection does not exist and that all human beings are imperfect.

3. Accept your weaknesses and imperfections, as well as those of others.

4. Focus your energy on your strengths and abilities, as well as those of others.

5. Celebrate every success or progress, even if they are imperfect.

This concludes the section on what to do to continue to improve yourself. Remember that your mistakes, your successes, the people you hang with, the opportunities you encounter, your search for excellence and your refusal to strive for perfection are the main things contributing to your improvement as a person and as a professional.

CONCLUSION

In short, to succeed in college you need to develop a winning attitude, respected skills and the best habits. These will help you get closer to your goals. Now you know the formula and its components:

COLLEGE SUCCESS = HABITS + SKILLS + ATTITUDE

How can you use this formula and these components in your studies?

- By understanding why they are important.
- By truly believing that they will pay off – and they will!
- By surrounding yourself with people who are better than you.
- By putting them into action today.
- By monitoring your progress.
- By rewarding every success.
- By persevering and believing in yourself!

Furthermore, not only is the combination of habits + skills + attitude a guarantee of success in college, but also in your career and in the other aspects of your life. Obviously, the same attitude and skills presented here are needed in all areas of life. But most of the habits I shared are related to academics and will need to be changed to fit your own professional and personal life. So even after graduation remember:

PERSONAL AND PROFESSIONAL SUCCESS

=

HABITS + SKILLS + ATTITUDE

I invite you to review and rewrite your goals for your career, such as who you want to become and what you want to accomplish.

Hopefully reading this book has motivated you and encouraged you that with good habits, skills and the right attitude, you can be and do more than you ever imagined.

Finally, I would like to share one last thought. Even if you feel pressured in your college classes and often behind in your work and your studies, realize that it is during college that you have the most time to develop your attitude, your skills and your habits. It is also during college that you have more opportunities available to you and you have more time to seize those opportunities and achieve them. So go for it! That is what will help make you a person of great value!

I wish you great success! I look forward to hearing from you and am so glad for the opportunity to contribute to your college success!

REMINDERS

*

Post On the Wall Next to Your Desk

and

Read It Every Week

- Be Responsible
- Control Your Education
- Visualize Your Goals
- Skim Through Your Course Material
- Understand Your Professors
- Read Each Day's Class Notes that Night
- Decide If Your Reading Assignments are Worth Your Time
- Select Key Material for the Rereading of Your Notes
- Understand the General Content of Your Classes
- Escape to a Secret Location Every Week
- Anticipate What Will Be on Your Exam
- Use Good Test-Taking Strategies
- Think Positively
- Schedule a Time to Work and a Time to Play
- Learn from Your Mistakes
- Avoid Perfectionism
- Remember : You Are Smart!

NOTES

1. Michael Geison, *How to Become A SuperStar Student*, 2nd Edition (The Teaching Company, 2011), DVD.

2. Paul R. Scheele, *Photoreading : Read with greater speed, comprehension, and enjoyment to absorb complete books in minutes* (Minnetonka, Minnesota: Learning Strategies Corporation, 2000), 163 pages.

3. Patrick S. O'Brien, *Making College Count: A Real World Look at How to Succeed In and After College*, 2nd Edition (Cincinnati, Ohio: Patrick O'Brien Enterprises, 2010), 250 pages.

ADDITIONAL REFERENCES

David Allen, *Getting Things Done: The Art of Stress-Free Productivity (London:* Penguin Books, 2001), 267 pages.

Susan H. Andreas and Felicity Pine, *Success in School: The Essential How-to Guide for Students of All Ages* (New York: Rowman & Littlefield Publishers, Inc., 2012), 77 pages.

Jack Canfield, *The Success Principles: How to Get from Where You Are to Where You Want to Be* (William Morrow Paperbacks, 2006), 512 pages.

Grace M. Charles, *Get to the Top of the Class: How to Succeed in High School; Your Personalized Guide to Academic Success* (New York: Gracie Mansion Publishing Corporation, 2009), 179 pages.

Stephen R. Covey, *The Seven Habits of Highly Effective People: Powerful Lessons in Personal Change* (New York: Simon & Schuster, 2013), 391 pages.

Rita Emmett, *The Procrastinator's Handbook: Mastering the Art of Doing It Now* (Walker Publishing Company, 2000), 192 pages.

Gunnar Fox, *Kick Ass in College: A Guerilla Guide to College Success*, 2nd Edition (Beaverton, Oregon: Kick Ass Media, 2013), 329 pages.

Dr. Marie M. Gilliam, *The Core Leadership Development Model* (Dynamic Leadership Solutions, LLC, 2009), 131 pages.

Jon B. Gould, *How to Succeed in College: A Professor's Inside Advice* (Chicago: The University of Chicago Press, 2012), 168 pages.

Dany Grimard and Josée Todd, *Cessez d'être bon, devenez excellent! L'indispensable guide pour propulser votre potentiel* (Un Monde Différent, Québec: Les éditions, 2013), 158 pages.

Cal Newport, *How to Win at College: Surprising Secrets for Success from the Country's Top Students* (New York: Three Rivers Press, 2005), 193 pages.

Sherrie Nist-Olejnik and Jodi Patrick Holschuch, *College Rules: How to study, survive and succeed in college*, 3rd Edition (New York: Ten Speed Press, 2007), 342 pages.

ABOUT THE AUTHOR

Dr. Jasmine Filion earned a Doctorate in Dental Medicine, graduating at the top of her class. During her postsecondary studies, she received several awards: Governor General's Academic Medal, International College of Dentists Award, the Natural Sciences Awards, the Oral and Maxillofacial Pathology Award, among others.

Jasmine is now not only a dentist, but also a sought-after tutor, mentor and speaker. Through her mentoring and tutoring, Jasmine coaches students on how to succeed in college by sharing her proven study strategies and helping them optimize their grades, extracurricular involvement and career opportunities. Through her speaking engagements in schools and other organizations, Jasmine shares her wisdom with parents, school counselors, as well as students.

Jasmine is the creator of the *University Success Formula Program*. In her program, Jasmine helps students build their unique personal plan for college success. She also coaches them through interactive activities presented in two different ways. Sometimes Jasmine shares her strategies with them and then her students do some exercises to apply the theory in their own life. At other times, Jasmine gives the students some exercises before they receive the theory, so the students make mistakes and learn from them. In her program, students learn individually as well as in groups.

Students have the chance to learn every single thing that most college graduates wish they had known before they started college. Her students have the chance to learn from a successful mentor, to build their personalized plan for success in college, and to learn from the mistakes they see other students make.

If you **wish** to learn more information about the *University Success Formula Program* or if you wish to book Jasmine as a speaker, you can email her: Jasmine@UniversitySuccessFormula.com.

Your are invited to LIKE the University Success Formula Book Page on Facebook:

https://www.facebook.com/universitysuccessformula

You are also invited to connect with Jasmine on LinkedIn: https://www.linkedin.com/pub/jasmine-filion/a2/833/269.

37502000R00147

Made in the USA
Charleston, SC
08 January 2015